CONSUMER PSYCHOLOGY
FOR
HUMANIZED BANK MARKETING

CONSUMER PSYCHOLOGY
FOR
HUMANIZED BANK MARKETING

MARTIN M. GROSSACK

With the Assistance of
Bruce McKinney
Robert Richmond

A Publication of the
Institute for Consumer Psychology
Hull, Massachusetts

Distributed by
Schenkman Publishing Company
Cambridge, Massachusetts

ALSO BY MARTIN GROSSACK:

Mental Health and Segregation
Understanding Consumer Behavior
Your Are Not Alone
Man and Men

CONTENTS

ACKNOWLEDGEMENTS

I should like to thank Dr. Gerald Leader for permitting us to use material from his research in Chapter Three of this work. Robert Richmond, the consulting industrial engineer of the Institute for Consumer Psychology, is responsible for Chapter Nine. Laurence McKinney, now presently with Media Engineering, Inc., helped write much of the work using material from the Institute's files. Peyton Galloway, now with Financial General Company, was very helpful to me while he was a second year student at the Harvard Business School.

I personally learned about banking from many others who know much more: Allan S. Beale, Frank McKeown, and Richard Peters at the Savings Bank Life Insurance Council of Massachusetts; Frank Christian and Ed Hickey at the New England Merchants National Bank; Al Baillargeon, Warren Berg, William Burtt, Walter Bush, John Kane, Lewis Perry, Lee Spelke, and James White at the National Shawmut Bank. I also should like to thank Dean Wolf and Myron Silton, experts on bank advertising, for the helpful insights they have given me.

Martin Grossack

PREFACE

This book should be viewed as a collection of articles, rather than as a unified presentation. As a commercial behavioral research firm, the Institute for Consumer Psychology wanted to present to the banking community some of the approaches it has developed and to illustrate their utility in practical business situations. We selected several areas in which our competence is most applicable:

1. The problem of winning and keeping customers through activities that occur inside the bank (Chapter One: *The Philosophy and Practice of Humanized Banking*);

2. The kind of officers traditionally employed in banks, how this is changing, and how the public sees bankers (Chapter Two: *How People See Bankers* and Chapter Three: *Bankers as a Social Type*);

3. The general approach of the consumer psychologist to the marketing and advertising problems of banks (Chapter Four: *Survey Methods* and Chapter Five: *Preliminary In-Depth Interviewing*);

4. Concrete examples of how banks utilize consumer psychology in their marketing and advertising (Chapter Six: *Increasing the Effectiveness of Bank Advertising,* Chapter Seven: *Researching the Psychology of Retail Banking,* and Chapter Eight: *A Study of Commercial Banking*);

5. Approaches for using industrial engineering in commercial banking (Chapter Nine: *Industrial Engineering for Banks*); and

6. Other problem areas worthy of consideration (Chapter Ten: *Bankers and the Community* and Chapter Eleven: *Concluding Comments*).

Banking is complex, and psychologists will find it a new field with exciting possibilities in personnel training and marketing, in helping bankers to meet the growing demands on their resources, and in increasing the effectiveness of their service to the business and retail publics. The ideas in this short book only begin to scratch the surface. Bankers will find it amusing in some parts, perhaps disconcerting in other passages, but hopefully useful as an entirety.

Institute for Consumer Psychology
Hull, Massachusetts
Dr. Martin Grossack, Director

INTRODUCTION

In the last ten years there has been an ever-increasing concern with the marketing activities of commercial banks, savings banks, trust companies, and other financial institutions. Yet it has taken a relatively long time for banking, as a profession, to begin to utilize the tools of marketing. This situation has been, to a large extent, the result of the rising economic picture in this country and the technological advances which have made much time-consuming activity require a fraction of the previous effort. Additionally, there is the important effect of electronic data processing and telecommunications in making information about banks rapidly available to large numbers of people who previously had no real conception of the role of the bank as a financial service and counseling center.

One of the most apparent results of these trends has been the emergence of a number of non-bank financial organizations. Unencumbered by tradition and history, these organizations have often been more ready to use consumer-oriented marketing techniques to inform and educate commercial and retail customers about their services. In 1900 banks controlled approximately 53% of the nation's financial business, but by 1952 this figure had decreased to 34% because of the inroads made by these non-bank financial intermediaries. Responding to this drop in their impact on the nation's financial affairs, banks finally began to make use of the marketing techniques which had previously been felt to be inappropriate to their conservative image. As banks began to remodel their public images, more creative and dynamic individuals began to find challenge and fulfillment in the financial profession; the result was an increase in the number of new banking positions. This, in turn, created competition which made the marketing aspect of banking assume an even more important role. In the fifties few banks would do more than insert short, conservative advertisements in magazines and newspapers. But now it is not uncommon to see imaginative television ads during prime evening time announcing the availability of money for automobile or other loans. Banks which had previously confined themselves to low-risk construction and home-improvement loans have responded to the increase in discretionary income in a variety of ways. Some banks offer free financial counseling. Others, recognizing that a trip to a foreign country is going to require large sums of money, have set up travel departments; if the customer is in reasonable financial condition they would like to be the ones to lend him that money.

The rapid increase in the marketing activities of banks, especially in the larger urban areas of the country, has brought its share of problems and misunderstandings. Some advertising agencies, accustomed to selling pancakes, were not aware of the image which potential customers wished to have maintained. Bank marketing departments, on the other hand, often found it difficult to break away from the stodgy conservatism which had typified the advertising of banks for so long. In the past few years there have been several books and a great many articles devoted to various subjects connected with bank marketing. Marketing research groups have attempted to offer their services, banks have recounted their successes and failures, and bankers themselves have written guides to more successful sales and marketing approaches.

During this time the Institute for Consumer Psychology has been actively involved in a variety of consumer surveys aimed at helping a number of banks gain a more complete knowledge of the audience to which they are directing their marketing efforts. It has become increasingly apparent to our staff that there is a communication gap which has to be bridged and re-bridged each time a contract is signed or a survey completed. Just as psychologists often make poor bankers, most bankers have difficulty understanding some of the work that psychologists are doing. Results have been obtained, which in turn led to successful marketing campaigns, but the reasoning behind many recommendations is often unclear.

This book is an attempt to help clear up the mystery which seems to surround the social psychologist in the minds of many bank officers and managers. Without going into tedious detail, we have assembled a number of chapters which deal with the fields of banking and consumer surveying, and with the way that each of the two professions can benefit by a clearer understanding of what the other is trying to do, including the tools and means through which interpretations are reached. We have examined the manner in which financial officers are viewed by outsiders. Further, we have made use of an excellent study by Dr. Gerald Leader which gives a great deal of insight into the matter of how bankers see themselves and how they react to various problems in their own environment. By way of further explanation, we have included a description of just what the social scientist is trying to find out when he does a consumer survey and the methodology he uses to gain the information he seeks. Finally, we have included two actual examples of how this work is done, the results obtained, and the manner in which these results helped to create more effective marketing and advertising programs.

This is neither the definitive book on banking for the use of psychologists, nor the definitive book on psychology for the use of bankers. It is, however, a step in the right direction. In short, this book is an attempt to make the work of the social scientist more understandable and helpful to a large segment of the business community, namely the financial professionals. It is the sincere hope of the authors that a more familiar knowledge of the science of consumer psychology will help the bank officer to take advantage of this field more readily and that as a result he will be able to promote more effectively the activities and the services of his bank to his business and retail customers, as well as to his community at large.

I
THE PHILOSOPHY AND PRACTICE
OF HUMANIZED BANKING

"I remember when I opened my first checking account. A friend of mine had one in a bank near our company and suggested that I go there. When I went to the main office of this bank, I was well dressed and felt quite proper. The bank was like a museum – very old looking – and the man who dealt with me was old and conservative in appearance, which was frightening to me. He seemed suspicious about why I would come to his bank. I mentioned my friend's name, and, of course, he did not know him. The bank was so big that it obviously was a great honor to have this fellow talk to me. He was polite enough, I suppose, but he questioned me about where I worked and made it seem like a priviledge to be accepted as their customer. I certainly did not feel comfortable there, but it was around 1950. I suppose they smile more now."

(From an interview with a middle aged executive)

This chapter will attempt to document this transition in bank outlook, and will describe a system which in a sense, can help to transform the typical bank into a customer-oriented business.

Banks *were* exclusive domains of the establishment. They selected their customers carefully and were not truly oriented to retail business. The masses of people saw them as stuffy, unfriendly, and distant. Today the competition for deposits and profit is intense and (as will be shown in subsequent chapters) the very kind of personalities in banking has shifted, as well as explicit policies recognizing that customers can be from every segment of the population.

In addition, there are intense pressures from the socially conscious urging banks to take community roles that do not lend always to operating profits. Today various ethnic types are found at the junior levels of bank staffs, and many whose accounts would not have been accepted in past years are now regular customers. Banks are increasingly afraid of public criticism, and, like politicians, are becoming oriented to public surveys and public relations.

5

One of the frequent games played by psychologists and sociologists is to have people rank occupations as to prestige. Before World War II the banking profession held one of the most prestigious positions in society. Today, though it still ranks high, the banking profession has dwindled in public prestige. The old motivations of job security and prestige are no longer enough to attract and keep the most imaginative and enterprising people in the executive ranks of banks. There is even difficulty in attracting the right people to jobs in the clerical and teller functions. And so banks are bending, becoming less aloof, and speedily entering the age of consumer psychology as consumer-oriented businesses. Marketing Departments are being established, studies commissioned, and new directions taken in public relations and advertising efforts. Instead of waiting for customers to enter their offices, banks are even sending credit cards to non-customers (sometimes without adequately checking the reliability of the recipient).

The new consumer-oriented philosophy of banks is one in which the bank no longer sees itself merely as a source of money. Banks now need to search the minds of the retail customer, to discover the wants of corporate presidents and treasurers, and to invent new services and approaches for keeping present customers and attracting new ones. The new advertising approach of banks is, therefore, one that impels the development of creative campaigns similar in flair and ingenuity to those advertising foods, tobaccos, soaps and automobiles.

One of the first goals of a bank has to be to find out who their present customers are in terms of age, sex, location, size of account, type of industry, services used, and potential for additional business. Many banks do not have their record keeping function set up to accomplish this basic objective without using new procedures in data collection and survey-taking.

Up until now, a lack of this consumer-oriented philosophy has hurt bank profits and has put credit unions, loan companies, mutual funds, and private investment counselors in more advantageous positions. The goal of humanized bank marketing is to make consumers more responsive to the bank itself as a financial guardian and counselor.

Consumer Psychology as an Agent of Bank Modification

The purpose of applying consumer psychology to banking problems is to find clear cut, concrete answers to business problems. Before the answers are found, the proper questions have to be asked, and the sources of these questions are:

1. Hunches of management
2. Comments by employees
3. Comments by customers

4. Observation of competitive activity
5. Hypotheses of the psychologist

One very important way to ask the proper questions is to have open-ended group interviews among the relevant retail publics of concern to the bank. Very often the questions raised and the directions indicated in these interviews may differ from and will supplement those supplied by management.

Finding answers to business problems is only one part of the process involved in helping a bank develop more suitable programs. The process also involves gaining an emotional involvement and commitment on the part of management to accept the research as a basis for *action*. Management must come to accept the statement of a famous psychologist, Kurt Lewin, who invented the concept of "action-research" . . . "no action without research, no research without action."

The implementation process in research involves working with personnel, calling officers, marketing departments, branch managers, computer people, tellers and the bank's advertising officers. The proper use of psychological services by banking involves a complex system of activities and decisions, one in which mistakes are frequent but whose overall results usually are fruitful.

The psychologist must combine his training in the behavioral sciences, his consulting skills, and this clinical acumen with practical experience in the business world. To be optimally effective the activities of the researcher must create the situational context and inter-personal communication from which imaginative new ideas and approaches may be created. In this sense, *the psychologist is an agent of change,* hopefully trained to respond to all the problems involved in getting people to do things differently. He must be tough skinned enough to deal with the natural resistances and tensions inherent in a commercial enterprise, but sensitive enough to support people who are learning new ways to deal with old as well as new issues.

The psychologist must be a communications specialist. His findings must be presented in clear and simple language. The emotional context of the presentation must be non-threatening, since in every bank there are people who resist new ideas, research, and outsiders. The psychologist does not make business decisions for the bank, but he provides the stimulus for new policy decision-making, for engendering innovation in a bank's internal functioning as well as in its selling and advertising.

Underlying Psychology in Commercial Banks

Most retail customers in the large city commercial banks are made to feel like the numbers on the bottoms of their checks. Banks need humanization in their everyday functioning at the inter-personal level. Banks are chilly, and they must become warm; they are aloof, and they must become personable. Bank advertising has warmed, but banks are still cold and aloof. People want personal relationship with their banks, but in actual practice these relationships do not exist. Bank officers do not know their retail customers; and banks are remiss in making the customer feel that he has someone at the bank to whom he can turn when there is a question.

It is not surprising that every bank experiences significant customer loss during a year. Customer loss drains the profit potential of a bank. The lack of a marketing orientation — a customer orientation that works — acts to keep a large percentage of the retail market fickle and unstable. This is quite apparent in cities where a large number of banks cluster in the same area. There is little difference among the banks in structure, layout, services rendered, and imaginative efforts designed to obtain the business of segments of the population. Customers frequently feel it doesn't matter where they bank and, more importantly, they tend to feel that the banks do not care about having their business.

The customer wants to feel important to the bank, especially in emergencies, and to receive friendly courtesy. Banks experience increasing difficulty in keeping their organizations functioning well. There is a large turnover of their most competent tellers and junior officers. In fact, many banks lose the most promising people to other professions and businesses. It is somewhat Utopian to hope that a bank could have the resources to offer a personal relationship to each retail customer. But the bank should be mindful that this is what people want.

The world is an anxious, uncertain changing place. But the bank has to project an atmosphere of stability, dependability, security, and comfort. Only a small number of retail customers will take the opportunity to develop personal relationships at their banks if their main banking activities concern checking or savings accounts, or loans. Today only a relatively few people will ask a banker for advice on insurance policies, tax returns, or travel plans unless these services are rendered more concretely. The alert bank should learn about the kinds of financial problems people need to solve. The alert bank will try to anticipate the future and offer services designed to fulfill these needs. It will evoke an image of an institution that is people-oriented and dedicated to the well being of the retail customer.

The Humanized Banking System

Basically, banks need to eliminate their image of being cold, stuffy, heartless institutions. They need to be seen as allies of the people and cooperative colleagues of the business community (large and small). This is especially true as the consumer protection movement grows, as radical elements are starting to shout "burn the banks," and as ethnic minorities see banks as a prime target for their frustration and blame them for social inequities and for lack of progress in combating poverty.

The Humanized Banking System is one small way to help customers and non-customers feel that they have a banking connection, This system gains new marketing data at a very low cost, lower than any other approach of studying a banks' clientele. It educates customers and cross-sells services so that the bank's investment is returned profitably and becomes self-liquidating. It promotes feelings of mutual obligation between bank and customer.

The bank must use a certain method for training an employee to implement the system. We help select the person to be trained. The results in sales alone pay the costs of the system. One bank tried this program with 387 people. Resulting sales included: an auto loan, eight checking accounts, eight charge cards, one personal loan, seven savings accounts, two revolving credit agreements and a bonafide lead for a $400,000 trust account. Mr. Galloway of our staff computed that the revenue produced from the loans on an annualized basis and the cost saved by the checking and savings accounts generated $1730 to the bank, far more than the salary paid to the employee. With this system the bank can see actual results daily, whereas with advertising it is hard to prove that a $100,000 budget generates 100 new accounts or additional sales. Therefore, we can confidently guarantee that any bank using the system will gain new sales.

This system involves personal contact with customers in a dignified manner. Banks have for too long relied on media advertising and on their reputation as sales tools, but research indicates that personal influence is the most important sales tool. (See Lazarsfeld 'Personal Influence," Free Press).

We help banks turn their lobby traffic into an asset, and we also provide a follow-up program. Special forms are used for tellers, bank employees trained by us, and platform people. The forms include simple to follow directions and systems of record keeping. The system develops word of mouth advertising and recommendations and softens the atmosphere of the bank.

The Humanized Banking System also enables the client bank to gain new marketing data about its customers and about the bank's competitive strengths and liabilities. It educates customers and cross-sells services. It humanizes the bank, develops goodwill, builds employee morale, and educates the staff in customer psychology. The system is designed to add warmth and glamour to banking. Humanized Banking creates new and stronger links to hold account acquisition circuits together and salvages high grade account opportunities that may otherwise go to competitors. Moreover, the development of this system, secures market data at a lower cost than conventional approaches to consumer research.

One bank using it reports: "Tangible results from this program were evident from the second day ... The idea and execution brought favorable comment from customers and prospects as well as from several business executives."

We are sure that in the future similar systems will be developed and improved. The main point we are making is that it is both easy and profitable to humanize banks of all types and sizes.

II
HOW PEOPLE SEE BANKERS*

Banks are Potentially Threatening

The typical client has less social status and prestige than the banker. In dealing with the bank he compares himself with the banker and wants acceptance. The bank must insure that the status of the individual is not threatened by his experiences there. The personnel can be trained to accept the client thoroughly, on a first name basis whenever possible, without lowering their own status level, i.e., by bring up the status of the client. In other words, the client should feel more important as a result of his every banking contact.

Psychological threat is most apt to occur in the borrowing situation. Here, to a limited extent in our data, the feelings of weakness and fear on the part of the client in contrast to the power of the banker seem most accentuated. Money is intimate and refusal implies lack of love and psychological rejection. Therefore, by having the client able to anticipate, prior to any request for a loan, how much money the bank can lend him when needed would prevent these unpleasant experiences from taking place. A client should, we think, know his credit potential at all times just as he knows his bank balance and how his credit limit is determined.

Again and again in the interviews, *banks are described as people:* the importance of having close friends at the bank is stressed. Basically, it is the *relationship* more than the services that leads to satisfaction with a bank.

Banker-Business Relationship

The relationship ideally suggested by our interviews is one in which the banker and businessman are interdependent (one partner need not be more

*From *Understanding Consumer Behavior,* edited by Martin A. Grossack, (Christopher Publishing House, 1966), pp. 291-297. (Originally published as "Product Areas Psychology and Commercial Banking.")

dependent than the other). It should be a closer relationship than many other business arrangements. This relationship should be cordial, on a first name level, and one in which the banker and businessman may be friends socially. However, the bank should always retain status.

The typical relationship is depicted as a very stable one that can be disrupted by only the most radical of events. A businessman wants to be loyal to his bank and to accept that it will make errors. In return, he expects loyalty from the bank and the assurance that he can borrow as easily in difficult circumstances as in ordinary circumstances.

A tendency was found for some executives to expect "fatherly" advice from the bank, especially if the businessman is young or needs to have his new ideas challenged by a more conservative person. Executives do not like to be on the asking end and to prove themselves deserving of loans. Here, a long-time client described his bank as acting in this way and felt that they should "unbend". The dimension of a "super-ego" that insures prudent decisions and avoids dubious activities for the businessman is the only feature of a father-figure that would be generally acceptable to this sample.

Rather, the relationship should generally be brotherly and helpful, but one of equals. However, we find variability in the feelings expressed by our sample concerning the relationship to the bank. This is due to personality differences in the sample and actual differences in the relationships found in the different local banks.

The businessman expects the banker to be an expert with specialized resources available for any need. He wants to feel that the bank wants and cares about his business and is devoted to its growth.

The relationship is described by a few respondents as a marriage . . . It is hard to break, one should not change banks too often, you can have confidence in the relationship.

On the other hand, some feel that the businessman must appear conservative, or dress especially well in order to receive the best treatment. Frequently, the feeling is expressed that the person would never be treated so well if he did not represent such and such a company. On the one hand, there are strong needs for individualized and preferential treatment. But business-men, we think, suspect the genuineness of the treatment they get since they feel that banks behave differentially to people depending on their firm and potential. One put it this way: "I am treated better because of whom I represent; others are treated in a *cold* business basis."

The relationship of businessman to banker is seen as a professional one with more integrity involved than other business associations and that is above reproach. It is *both* a business and personal relationship. It seems more closely associated to an attorney than to a physician in that the relationship to the physician is seen as more intimate and the physician is seen as too busy for the personalized relationship one might expect of a bank. As one respondent put it: "A bank is people," and it is our opinion that the people should be advertised.

Utilities are seen as monopolies. However, utilities are generally seen favorably in terms of the services. A few respondents did verbalize hostility towards the Telephone Company and negative comments concerning monopolistic behavior were given by some. However, one individual felt that utilities were more approachable than banks. Utilities are seen as lesser monopolies. The bank relationship is, of course, seen as a more personal one and the bank is seen as selecting its clientele, which utilities can not do.

Regarding insurance companies, the relationship there seems affected by whether or not you deal with an independent broker or the company directly. The relationship with the broker would parallel that of the banker more closely than a relationship with the company directly.

Banker Personality

The study revealed feelings as to the personality characteristics expected in a banker. Although respondents could repeat cartoon stereotypes of bankers as "pompous, overstuffed, and portly, cigar-smoking at a big desk while frowning at people", the executives had definite expectations of the kind of person they would expect to represent a bank. The traits looked upon with favor were:
1. The banker should be of an upperclass background, giving the impression of a substantial citizen who is respectable and who would give prestige to the client.
2. The banker should be well-educated.
3. He should be active in community projects, e.g., The United Fund.
4. He should be personally conservative in his tastes and private life, but an aggressive businessman with exceptional business ability.
5. In appearance, he should be tall, dignified, well-dressed, and a good talker.
6. A banker should be male.
7. He should be easy to talk to in a professional manner.
8. He should be similar in age and background to the client, suggesting that a variety of personality types be employed to appeal to the variety of client personalities.
9. He should be cordial, always ready to serve the client and do anything possible to help him.

Emotional Meaning of Banks

For the typical businessman, banks are a status evaluator. The bank has more status and prestige than the businessman. Therefore, every contact with the bank puts one's status open to evaluation. In the projective items, frequent feelings are reported that "bankers feel I am a small depositor" or "I am too small to be bothered with". Therefore, there is a reluctance to go to banks on the part of some businessmen.

The bank is a power symbol, and, thus, the individual needs the bank more than the bank needs him. There is consequently a fear of inconsiderate ego-deflating treatment that would make the client feel unimportant. The businessman wants to feel close to the banker and at home with him. Therefore, a middle-sized company could feel more important to a smaller bank, just on the basis of size. The value of using a commercial bank, *that is not so large that it becomes impersonal,* could be stressed by smaller banks.

These feelings and needs become apparent in the comparisons businessmen make between banks in the past and banks today. In the past, banks are described as having been dictatorial, pretentious, and holier-than-thou in attitude. They gave hard, impersonal, and unkindly treatment. Bankers are described as now being more natural and down to earth, aggressively seeking business, and willing to bargain. Regionally, banks outside of New England are described as warmer, more ambitious and aggressive. However, one respondent associates the success of the New England banker with his conservative perfectionistic approach to business.

Choosing a Bank

The study revealed that banks are selected as a result of social influences and decisions are not purely economic or psychologically based. Again and again, the importance of *word of mouth* influence is stressed.[1] Businessmen frequently select the bank for their business in terms of influences by their own circle of associates. This is especially important for influencing new companies, since many firms, due to company tradition, are extremely unlikely to change connections. Therefore, it would be wise for a bank to work on present clients to obtain new ones through personal recommendations.

An example is given of a company moving to a small town in the Midwest and needing a banking connection in the town. The President asked his associates in the town about the banks in town that they used. Then, he visited each with a definite preference for one before his visits were made. Ultimately he selected the one suggested by his friends. Another example was given of how an executive's wife influenced choice of banks.

[1] See W. H. Whyte, "The Web of Word of Mouth," *Fortune*, November 1954.

Commercial Banks Need an American Image

Psychological literature provides us with lists of the twelve traits most frequently assigned to English and Americans:

English	*Americans*
sportsmanlike	industrious
intelligent	intelligent
conventional	materialistic
tradition-loving	ambitious
conservative	progressive
reserved	pleasure-loving
sophisticated	alert
courteous	efficient
honest	aggressive
industrious	straight-forward
nationalistic	practical
humorless	sportsmanlike

The depth interviews suggest that businessmen want bankers *personally* to be conservative, in manner but progressive, aggressive and straight-forward in their business practices. In this respect, the commercial banks need to change their image to fit the stereotype of Americans more closely than the English.

*Revised from Martinn M. Grossack's *Understanding Consumer Behavior* (Christopher Publishing House, 1966), pages 291-97.

III
BANKERS AS A SOCIAL TYPE

In our role as social scientists we continually observe how people feel, think, and behave, and we then use these observations to suggest plans of action which harmonize expectations and reality. When we are under contract to study a consuming group, we have questions for those for whom we work as well as for those whom we are studying. If an individual cannot stand apple pie, there is no use in our researching why his customers like apple pie because there is little chance that the two will ever reach a workable agreement about its value.

So it is with social types and mannerisms. Although there do exist retiring salesmen and aggressive professors, there are definite characteristics regarded as typical and natural for certain jobs and professions. In most cases these characteristics result from the demands of the job, but in some situations the traditional nature of the task, together with it's usual life style, attracts people of a certain personality type. There is probably a reason for the unusually high percentage of introverts among psychoanalysts. A psychoanalyst is constantly exposed to troubled minds, and he must remain withdrawn enough to be able to offer objective assistance. Many individuals would find it very difficult to resolve this tension between the desire to help and the necessity to remain distant, but there are certain people – many of them psychoanalysts – who see this frustration as a fitting challenge to their ability to keep a level head under strained circumstances. How well they practice their craft is a matter of individual talent; the fact that they have chosen this particular profession from among many is still a matter of interest.

This situation is the same in all professions. (We make the distinction of "professions" here, since there are a great many people who simply work at a job because they have to earn money, whereas most "professionals" have chosen a job to their liking.) There is a type of personality associated with the clergy, with academic life, with business management and with the financial professions. Within the financial professions, there are a good many differences between the broker, the stock market specialist, the leading member of an investment banking firm, and the commercial banker. In this chapter, we will attempt to investigate the social type most commonly associated with commercial banking and to understand how, under the pressures of a changing world, this type of person seems to be shedding the traditional mannerisms and styles so long associated with bankers.

More than ten years ago, in June, 1958 Robert N. McMurry published an article in the *Administrative Science Quarterly* entitled "Recruitment, Dependency, and Morale in the Banking Industry." This report was a summary of the conclusions McMurry had reached after some nine hundred interviews with banking and investment-house employees, six hundred of whom were given several carefully structured, detailed tests to evaluate their abilities and values. In his article McMurry pointed out that the study led to the same general conclusions usually assumed by popular culture. Banks on the whole were extremely conservative, autocratic, and uncompetitive institutions in which the "right type" individuals worked quietly and meticulously and were usually rather meek, fastidiously dressed, security-minded, and dependent. Dependent in this sense did not mean untalented or unable, but merely the opposite of independent, i.e., those people who were more than usually respectful of delegated authority and inclined to seek consultation before making any important decisions. McMurry concluded his article:

> ... If banks are to meet increasing competition both among themselves and with outside agencies, for example, small loan chains, mutual funds for savings and so on, they must recognize that employees of the "right type" are not going to keep them competitive. Banking must become more dynamic and aggressive. It can no longer survive on its dignity as an "institution."

Bearing in mind the dramatic changes which have taken place in the banking world within the last ten years, it is easy to discount such a pessimistic view as not accurately taking into account the ability of financial professionals to sense changes in the market place and adapt accordingly. This adaptation has, however, not always been either easy or smooth, and today there is a dramatic contrast between banks of the old style and banks of the new. In 1965 Gerald C. Leader conducted a thorough study of the situation, centering his investigations on a particular bank which was apparently in the process of becoming a dynamic and aggressive financial institution. He recorded his findings in a doctoral thesis written for the Harvard Graduate School of Business and entitled "The Determinants and Consequences of Interpersonal Competence in a Bank Setting." In the next few pages we often will refer to this work because it has provided some provocative insights into the manner in which bankers tend to see themselves, how they view their business and social roles, and how there have come to be several different sorts of "bankers" within a profession which McMurry felt was comprised of only one general type.

Social scientists often use general classifications such as "task specialists" and "social specialists." Both can be found within any business environment, along with the "generalist." The most fundamental difference between the specialists and the generalists is the way in which they measure their own self-esteem. The need for this self-esteem varies greatly among individuals and has been subject to measurement recently in the many works dealing with motivational psychology. This motivation may be examined by a "need achievement" test, which attempts to measure the need within an individual to be successful. But it is not specific as to the means, recognition, or the roles of other persons in the process of achieving this success. The level of "need achievement" varies from individual to individual, and, depending on one's orientation as a task specialist, a social specialist or a generalist, the manner of achieving success is viewed in entirely different ways.

Both task specialists and social specialists seem to direct themselves towards immediate and discrete tasks rather than long-term generalized goals. Task specialists, however, appear to have a higher "need achievement," whereas the social specialist has a high preference for status. This would indicate that the typical task specialist identifies his self-esteem with excellence in his work, whereas the social specialist is more oriented towards recognition by others than towards pure achievement. The inherent problem with either sort of specialization is that each tends to overlook the other side of the coin to its own disadvantage. In Arthur Miller's *Death of a Salesman* it becomes obvious that Willy Loman's overriding desire to be "well-liked" and his fruitless attempts to instill this goal in his sons were key factors in his eventual downfall. He tried so hard to be well-liked that he failed at his actual business goal, which was to be a good salesman. The loss of his job hastened Willy's collapse when he could not bear to face the fact that being "well-liked" does not insure personal success. And yet, we are all too familiar with the hard working task specialist who neglects friendships and social responsibilities alike in his dogged pursuit of his work. Generalists, on the other hand, seem to indicate that they do not identify achievement and self-esteem with immediate task accomplishment. Unlike either of the "specialists," they are likely to generalize their measurements of achievement. Neither social recognition nor finite "work" is considered an end in itself.

Both types of "specialists" have certain difficulties working with people, but the difficulties are very different. The task specialist typically feels a need to exert influence, while at the same time he does not enjoy working with other people. The social specialist needs to work with people and does not attempt to influence, preferring to accept the direction of others. Banks, it seems, are usually populated with specialists who work these complementary needs and defences against each other in such a way as to maintain their *status quo* without ever really having to pay much attention to the customer with whom they are in daily contact. Until recently this mode of behavior was quite sufficient to maintain a smooth-running bank. The pressures of the sixties and the seventies, however, with the greatly increased supply of discretionary income in the hands of consumers, as well as the more active business climate, have created a far more competitive situation. Money and financial services are more eagerly sought, for more reasons and by more people. The more aggressive individuals are beginning to take active roles in the policy-making decisions of up-until-now staid and conservative operations. Many of these activities may be contrasted directly with McMurry's pessimistic analysis:

> The routine nature of the majority of the operations in a bank, with their major emphasis on checks and balances makes the total structuring of each activity almost inevitable. Even in extending credit, bankers have well-established standards to guide them, for example, the current ratios, capital ratios, inventory ratios, sales ratios, and net profit ratios. Except at the very top levels of management, no decision-making exercise of judgement or risk-taking of consequence is required of anyone. In the intermediate levels a committee usually decides. Every contingency has been provided for. In the rare instances that an unusual situation arises, a superior is available to consult – and to approve the action to be taken. [Thus] all but the most senior positions require mainly diligence, conscientiousness, and a proper respect for constituted authority.

Mr. Abel, the new president of the bank which was the focus of Leader's thesis, worked to counter McMurry's view. Mr. Abel's prescriptions for how he had attempted to organize the internal activities of his bank were in almost complete contrast. But from his remarks, it was obvious that these changes had not met with complete acceptance.

Mr. Abel: *You know banking has a funny idea about taking risks. In the business community as a whole, people don't mind using trial and error, that is, introducing new products; and then if the product doesn't work out, they let it go and try something else. But bankers think that they must play errorless ball. They think that they have to follow age-old principles and not experiment with new programs. But I am of a different persuasion; for* *example, we try a lot of different approaches with our advertising, and sometimes these approaches haven't worked out well. I've spent as much as $30,000 on a program that flopped. We try to introduce services, and if they don't work out, we let them fall and work out something else. We don't shout it from the housetops that we have made an error, but we don't shoot the person for making that error. Bankers try to create the impression that they are infallible, but don't you think for a second that they foist that image on the public, because I don't think anyone believes it, including themselves. What I am trying to say is, we don't take it too hard if a program fails, but we really 'lean hard' on the ones who fail to get up and get going at all . . . We are awfully hard on people who don't try anything. I try to encourage innovative behavior.*

Although bankers of Mr. Abel's type are more common than they were ten or twenty years ago, they are still in a definite minority. This fact becomes particularly important when one focuses the question on the effectiveness of certain personality types in dealing with clients. Again, we refer to McMurry's conclusion as to the general attitudes of the traditional bank officer:

> Senior bank officers usually enjoy a position of special prestige and distinction in their communities. Not only are they regarded as authority figures, comparable to the physician and the clergyman, but in their day to day business dealings they tend to be in a superior status position (as contrasted, for example, to that of a salesman who is essentially a suppliant) as a result of their economic power over the borrower. Such circumstances can create in the bank officer an exalted conception of his importance and omniscience and can foster the growth of any inherent authoritarian tendencies. The very elegance of many banking houses and of the officer's quarters in them, and the awe they create in the average citizen may contribute further to the banker's idealized conception of himself.

With respect to external relationships, Mr. Abel had quite a different set of ideas as to how a bank officer should operate:

> *In my estimation, banking is a process of dealing with people. There are the financial aspects of the problem, of course, but in essence it is dealing with people. For example, if I, a bank officer, receive a hundred calls a day, ninety-nine of them will be from people who want me to do something for them. That's axiomatic. I would be stupid to think otherwise. Banking is a service*

institution, and the officers of the bank should have the posture of wanting to serve the public. Of course, we also have the responsibility to protect against losses and keep the money secure . . . A policy I've instituted is that it takes one to say yes *but two to say* no *to any particular proposal of a customer. Do you know that I recently had to talk with several officers who said that they had not said no to a customer, when in fact the customer had gone to another bank and gotten a loan. They wouldn't tell me directly that they had turned down a customer when in essence that was what they did. They made it so complicated and complex and put in so many rules and provisions on the terms of the loan that they in fact turned the customer down. A lot of the officers just don't realize this. Moreover, a lot of the officers don't realize that a lot of the people coming into a bank to ask for a loan ask to be accommodated in a very forceful manner, but, in fact, underneath them their knees are shaking.*

There used to be a policy in at least two of the banks that we have merged with, and it had been a policy in the banking houses for a number of years, one which is followed in most institutions, that a client would make a proposal, then later a committee would give a yes or no answer on the proposal. But I can't think of a more stupid way of handling the situation. A good banker gathers together the facts himself, finds out what the customer wants, and then gives the customer what he needs, as is most advantageous to the bank and to the customer. This is to be contrasted with an officer saying to the customer, "I looked over your financial situation, and this is exactly what you need." . . . because in many cases this is just a rationalization to give him the plan that the banker had already drawn up in his head previously. People don't like a finger waved at them or being told what they need.

If there is anything banking has to sell, there is service, and a good banker will look at any particular customer problem and look at it in all its aspects. That is, he will gather all the information together and then try to come up with a plan that will do more for the customer within the bank's policy. If the proposal isn't originally satisfactory to the customer, an alternative should be given that compromises the objectives of the customer and the bank. Rarely, and I do mean rarely, should a flat no be given to the customer. Of course, this is not to say that a flat no should not be given to a swindler or a high-handed wheeler dealer, these types you try to get out of the bank just as fast as possible.

I'm trying to orient this organization to become very customer-minded in their approach. The officer's job is no longer the storekeeper's job where they come to you for five pounds of sugar and you send them on their way without selling them scissors or a pound of flour. Moreover, we are not exclusively selling groceries over the counter, we have to sell our products by going out to the customers.

The contrasts between the situation McMurry describes and that which Mr. Abel is attempting to implement could not have been more complete. No longer does Mr. Abel condone the disproportionate balance of power which the officer once held over the client. Even if the prospective customer suppliantly comes to the bank for financial help, the officer cannot, as far as Mr. Abel is concerned, arbitrarily turn him down — the ultimate essence of the officer's previously held power. Instead, he must do everything possible to make an agreement which is acceptable to both the bank and the client. In short, a bi-lateral officer-client relationship is being advocated. What is most interesting and hopeful is that Mr. Abel explicitly calls attention to the need for both kinds of behavior in the officer-client relationship. For example, with the absence of any sort of client rapport, the officer's attempt to influence can be viewed by the customer as "finger waving" and [Mr. Abel observes] "people don't like to have fingers waved at them and to be told what to do." On the other hand, the officer cannot rely solely on the maintenance of a close relationship with the client. "High-handed and wheeler-dealer types have to be dealt with firmly and emphatically." However, the officer must use influence, albeit subtle influence, in selling alternative proposals to the client should the one originally proposed be incompatible with the bank's general policies. In Mr. Abel's words, "You can't send them on their way without selling them a pair of scissors or a pound of flour."

Needless to say, a bank president such as Mr. Abel is no longer the rarity he once was. It seems, however, that he was enough ahead of the times so that he was unable to get reasonable cooperation from the original personnel of the bank. Finally, he was able to train and install a new management team which raised the bank's assets almost seventy percent over a ten year period. Even recognizing the fact that some of this growth was the result of a successful merger with another bank, the internal growth rate was far above that of any other bank in the area.

Common sense would indicate that methods of operating a business which, when measured in dollars and cents, were clearly superior to the accepted traditional methods would be enthusiastically welcomed by reasonable men of business. Unfortunately, few men anywhere are actually reasonable, especially when it comes to custom. If one way of doing things has been proper and profitable in the past, most individuals are naturally reluctant to embark on an entirely new posture when working in an area they feel well acquainted with. One often underestimates, however, just how much of the emotional security of doing things in a traditional manner is a reflection of the individual's own personal sense of values rather than the values which ought to be assigned to the work which he does.

In later interviews with other members of the staff of Mr. Abel's bank, Leader was able to uncover a strong tenacity in some individuals to generalize all customers in such a way that a meaningful officer-client rapport would be very difficult to achieve no matter what the particular circumstances were. We want to remember at this point the earlier classification of task specialists; those who see the task as the most important aspect of their business life and, provided that the task is well-defined to begin with, will rely on predetermined guidelines and tend to be less observant of the actual details of a situation. These details might require original judgement and new decision-making rather than the application of "tried and true" formulas for an efficient job well done.

Leader makes the following observations: "That a prevalent professional ethic [existed at Mr Abel's bank] would not be the concern of this research if it were not for the fact that a large number of [the bank] officers used it as an authority, albeit surreptitiously, in justifying their resistance to changes which have been taking place at the bank. In fact, there is good reason to presume that this either would be impossible to codify if it were not for the conflict which the professional *sees* between the ways he believes he *should* behave and the way Mr. Abel is 'forcing' him to behave. There is nothing which is more capable of bringing out a person's latent predispositions, values and ideals than threatening the actualization of satisfaction.

The two (types of specialized behavior) drew scattered adherents from across the total population (of bank employees) but were mainly concentrated in two separate departments of the bank, where the norms supporting these schisms were particularly powerful. The locus of the technical (task) professionalism was in the credit and loan department, while the locus of service professionalism approximated the boundaries of the cashier department and, in a more limited way, the trust department. Essentially, the two groupings have seized on the two major components of the professional ethic. The professional does "technically competent work" in one instance and he "services the client" in the other, and he has blown up these two modes so out of proportion that in the end each subverts the other." In the situation which was the focus of Dr. Leader's study, these two areas of specific expertise were made even more distinct by the persuasive presence of Mr. Abel, the "generalist" who was now the president of the bank.

Leader was able to collect some very revealing interviews with representatives of both types of behavior. In these interviews it becomes apparent that the individual presenting his opinions is really quite influenced by behavior patterns which seem perhaps unsuitable for a man engaged in a business which relies on a mutual understanding between the client and the bank.

Loan Officer "A":   *There is no doubt that experience is the most important factor in this game. Anyone with a little training can read a balance sheet or an income statement, but it takes someone with experience to make decisions based on the* facts *on the financial information. . . . Also you have to have the experience of* handling *people. . . . At the end of our financial analysis we certainly know a lot about the principal of the firm. . . . You know the* worst enemies *in this business are your* friends, *because you are* not firm enough *with them. You let them get by, say a month, when the loan payment is overdue, and then it goes on another month, and then another month and you just can't be firm enough with them. With all the advertising the bank is doing, saying that we are friends of everyone brings in all types of people. But I've been in this business for over twenty-five years, and it's got so now that a person can sit down next to my desk and* before he opens his mouth, *I can tell whether he is a* phoney *or not. Everyone gets his day in* court, *however, and we listen to anybody who wants to come in here and talk about a loan. If we can't give him a loan, we at least* let him believe *that he had a* sympathetic ear.

Loan Officer "C":   *Yes, I would say that my mind works in such a way that it enjoys tackling large, poorly defined problems and then, by deduction, putting the components into* manageable compartments *and then developing a logical sequence in solving the problem... Also you have to be good at analyzing people to be a good loan officer. I've seen some very intelligent and very personable people who have failed at this kind of work because they could not make adequate judgements of other people. This aspect of the work is really somewhat of a strain, but it's very important.... An extroverted person who is very desirous of making and keeping human relationships can really have a hard time; it takes a great deal of* personal stamina to turn one's back on a friend, *but sometimes it's quite necessary. Frequently, the case arises where a person who you once* liked *has to be 're-viewed' in a new light and this may very well be as a* bad man.... *To a very large extent, the loan officer has to* build a wall around himself *and* cut himself off from other people. *Sometimes you have to* let the bars down *in order to go out and work for more business.*

What is interesting is the similar and precise manner in which these gentlemen have delineated their job, and particularly the limits they have set on the kind of relationship they will have with their clients. No human sentiment will be a part of the interaction (i.e., before he opens his mouth I can tell whether he is a phoney or not, . . . "the loan officer . . . has to cut himself off from other people"). In this regard, friendship and work are not to be mixed, because it is difficult to "turn one's back on a friend." Moreover, the differential status relationship will at all costs be maintained ("day in court" and "let the bars down"). In their view, the client comes to the officer for help, and the help he dispenses has a rational and technical basis.

It is relatively unclear which is the cause and which is the effect, but the maintenance of an objective distance between himself and his clients and the maintenance of a technical orientation toward his work are both strongly linked in the professional's mind. At the particular bank discussed, it might again be stressed that some of this emphasis may have been in reaction to the presence of Mr. Abel's directives to become more involved with the client and to try to wrangle something out of the relationship which would be of value to both bank and client.

Leader notes that there are rather obvious psychological defenses evidenced which block the officers from establishing any sort of sympathetic rapport with a client. Another loan officer quoted had this to say:

It's pretty well impossible to say just what goes into making a good man for this type of work. In the old days banks were thought of as cold places. It was wrong to borrow money and consequently people thought it was wrong to go into banks, if you had to borrow something, this was wrong. Now when banks started to change this, they started to advertise that the bank was a friendly place. Later on, banks found that competition was increasing and they found that they had to 'stick up' to the customer. Everyone found that it was easier to sell banking services by getting close to the customer. *I believe the whole thing is completely overdone. . . . I personally don't like to talk about a* friendly banker *just like I don't like to talk about a* friendly mortitian. *You don't have to be a friend or close to your client, that's not a loan officer's function, it's to make a good account for the bank.* It's impossible for a banker to be friendly with everyone. *Three people are coming into a bank and asking for a loan; two you can give a loan to and one you can't. For the two who received loans, you are a fine guy, and for the other you are an old meany. Even when you play the* treacherous middle ground *you still come out as an old enemy.*

"The professional asks the client to believe in him, but" Leader explains, "he is unwilling to trust the client. That is, by failing to establish any sort of close rapport with the client, the officer cannot help but look upon the client with skepticism and mistrust. Although the banker is attempting to follow the model of the doctor and the lawyer, his financial involvement with the client prevents him from *not* caring about what the client does with his advice and suggestions. When it comes right down to it, the loan officer is aware that he is indeed responsible for what happens with the funds that he loans, or the accounts he approves. But too often it seems that to avoid as much of this personal responsibility as possible, he will attempt to concern himself solely with the "facts" of the matter and the technical information, which he feels he can deal with, rather than the complexities of human nature. "Thus, at least for some officers," Leader maintains "the professional ethic provides a ready justification for maintaining a rather rigid and specified relationship with their clients."

Although he recognizes that there is always a danger of overgeneralizing, Leader believes that "the evidence in the preceding cases is fairly clear and could be further documented. The establishment of a bi-lateral bargaining position between officer and client is being thwarted by some strong personal needs and defenses." There is no question that a certain amount of detachment is necessary in doing a practical job, but there are some aspects of banking which require a personality which is open and warm to the client. When a man is applying for a business or a personal loan he is psychologically ill at ease simply because he knows he may not receive the money which he feels he needs. At a time like this, a man who will listen quietly and sympathetically and offer constructive advice is far more likely to keep the customer as a client even if the original request cannot be met.

As there is the danger of being overly "task-oriented," there has always been the problem of being too much on the other side as well. In a banking situation, this disparity between personality types becomes especially obvious since the "anti-technical professional" sees himself in the vanguard of modern, friendly banking just as the "technical professional" idealizes his style of business as the only manner appropriate for a financial officer. A balanced individual is the most competent in building and maintaining new businesses. In the search for a more aggressive style, banks at times find themselves burdened by the sort of man who is, just like the "task specialist," more oriented towards maintaining what he considers the "right style" than in furthering the general and specific goals of the bank. As Leader discovered in the bank where he did his study, "there exists at [the bank] a group of officers who, though proportionately smaller in number compared to the 'professionals,' take as their ethos the negative or opposite statement of the professional ideal. Technicalness, social and emotional restraint, mistrust and differential status maintenance, characterize the professional's relationship with his clients; the use of social skills, free and easy social exchange and the desire to take risks characterize these individuals. By their own admission, they derive their ethos not so much from the positive statement of an ideal, but from a reaction against the professional." Thus, they can justifiably be called anti-professionals. A particularly articulate exponent of this school of thought had this to say:

> It's extremely easy to take a prudent position in your loaning policy and make minimum risk loans, but in order to be a really good loan officer you have to take risks *much in the same way a gambler takes a risk at the roulette wheel. As far as I'm concerned, and I know this would be* considered heresy *by most people, you place your bets and just see how the ball bounces. . . . There are some sleepless nights and extra work with this attitude, but this is what it takes to be a good loan officer. Sure it is easy to duck some loans because the*

risk is fairly great, but this is where the money is made. Lending is not a science *and if anyone tells you this, they are all wet. If it were, you could plug the variables into a computer and get a decision. It's just not that easy. In this business you sometimes have to be utterly ruthless. You have to be able to* stand the heat, *or you might as well get out, put yourself on the platform, and do nothing but initial Travellers Checks. Some people have to take platform work in order to sleep, because if you can't stand the heat and sleep, too, then you are in a sad shape.*

I've got a real hot loan going with a real estate operator who is as slippery as they come. He plays it very close; last week he was in here asking for an additional line of credit with no specific projects mentioned and his debt was already too high. I got a little mad and criticized *him.* But this guy was sophisticated enough to come *right back at me. He said, 'do you want me to tell you fairy tales or do you want met to tell you what I'm actually going to do with the money which is to pay off the balance of another loan down in New York?'* Even though *this breaks every rule in the book, I went along with him, I've been doing business with this guy for a couple of years and* he's *never let me down. If you pin him down on a matter and ask him why he has done something or what he is going to use the money for, he usually has a very good explanation.* There is very rarely not a meeting of the minds between us. *But practically* everyone here at the bank thinks I'm an idiot to keep this one on.

As Leader explains, "there are several general points in the above statement which are representative of this general category of bank officers. First, the officer assumes a bargaining posture in his relations with the client. The relationship is one of equals sitting down together working out an agreement. Second, given this kind of relationship, there is a necessity on the part of the officer to influence and be influenced — to be critical and take criticism. But the tensions created by these exchanges are contained within the relationship and are dissipated in the close rapport which exists between the parties. Third, the officer assumes that the client will 'come clean' if he, the officer, 'comes clean' with him. Indeed, a good portion of the solidarity between the parties is based on mutual trust. The officer, once having assured himself of the clients integrity and business acumen, will remain staunchly loyal to him, despite criticism he receives from his colleagues. Hence, the essence of these individuals' skills is not so much technical as it is interpersonal. Moreover, their unique hallmark is a client- rather than colleague-orientation, and the taking of risks is their *cause celebre*."

When a bank assumes a more aggressive image, officers like these become the stars of the show. The major difficulty, of course, is in reinforcing rather than tempering negative attitudes, there is the possibility that such individuals may periodically get carried away. Every bank has those officers, or ex-officers, who were just perfect as image-builders but whose occasional lack of judgement on one or two small decisions cost the bank considerable amounts. At the bank under study a particular loan officer had to be fired after he had made too many loans which had defaulted. The cost to the bank was not severe, but it did considerable damage to the attempts of the new president to instill a more "people oriented" style among his officers.

"To professionally oriented senior officers, " Leader observes, "[this man's] failings provided a ready and obvious justification for maintaining, indeed reinforcing, their traditional patterns of behavior. To the junior officers at the bank, his firing intensified the dangers already seen to be inherent in becoming too close to one's client and taking on anything but the safest loan agreements. Typical of the first reaction are the remarks of a senior loan officer who spoke of [the dismissed officer] as follows:

> *We had a man here at the bank who by nature was friendly with everyone; I called him a St. Bernard with no discretion. He would literally kiss the burglars. He always believed everything that anyone told him. His indiscretion darned near killed the bank. He has some little link missing in his computer which shorted out all discretion. That little light in his computer just didn't blink."*

Where the senior officer displayed a solid "I-told-you-so" attitude, bolstering his ability to maintain his own impersonal style, some younger officers were intimidated by the event so that they became distrustful of their own abilities to handle decision-making problems on their own.

> *I really enjoy the work I am doing now . . . I guess you would call it a worthwhile job. . . . I do most of Mr. X's legwork, and he discussed with me the particular pro's and con's of a loan decision. Once in a while he lets me take off my 'academic hat' and we go over together just how a financial analysis applies in a particular decision. I*

> have no desire to go out on my own at this particular
> stage of my career. I'm trying to build up a solid base of
> experience. Some of my colleagues have tried to go out
> on their own too early, and they have been hurt by it.
> Once you get a reputation around here as a "marginal
> loaner" it's hard to live it down. There is a real
> temptation for people who do not watch themselves to
> take on too much responsibility, go berserk, and just
> give the money away.

Despite the reactions to the demise of the "indiscrete" loan officer, there were some officers in the bank who did not view the situation in a black-and-white manner. Their actual behavior was similar in style to the "anti-professionals," except for the impression of calm self-assurance they left with clients. One such officer, who was rated very high by the bank's management on all performance criteria, discussed his lending philosophy as follows:

> I think there are two distinct schools of thought on
> lending philosophy. Mr. B. (one of the interviewed
> 'professionals') is as good an example as any on the one
> side. He is very much a technician and follows the rules
> very closely. When he goes to make a loan, he gathers all
> the available financial information and then does not
> make a hasty decision, but ponders it for some time.
> That is not to say that he is not an imaginative lender.
> He is a very imaginative person and although all his loans
> are not the grand and excellent variety, most of them are
> substantial, and once in a while he makes a very good
> one. I guess the other school can best be represented by
> the dismissed officer. He was a very nice guy, and I
> really liked him, but he made most of his loans "by the
> seat of his pants." A guy would come in the bank and
> say "I'm a friend of Joe Blow" and he would know that
> Joe Blow was a good guy, and so he would give the guy a
> loan. Of course it wasn't just like that. He would first
> size the guy up, looking him over pretty thoroughly, but
> looking the guy over was about the extent of his
> analysis. It not only generated a lot of deposits, but it
> created an intense loyalty to this man, and it brought a
> lot of business into the bank. I guess I fall somewhere
> between these two positions. When I first came to the
> bank, the "star" of the loan officers was Mr. X. He was

*the hot shot of the whole operation, and I envied him. I
still hold his approach as my model, but my own
philosophy has changed a little since then. I believe I've
become more careful, more particular in my loans.
However, I don't want to become too particular. . .*

According to Leader, "This balanced, integrated stance of the young
officer also is carried over into his attitudes towards his clients. Like the
anti-professional, he manifests a definite outward orientation; that is, his
loyalties are basically with his clients rather than with his colleagues. Yet,
contrastingly, there is not in evidence the hurried 'get rich quick' mode which
has caused financial difficulties for so many other anti-professionals. His is a
longer term and more thoughtful strategy.

*Most of the new business that comes my way is
indirectly through word of mouth of my present
customers. If I do a good job for them, they spread the
word around that I am a good loan officer. Then,
secondly, I am cultivating the friendship of several
young lawyers here in the area. Usually lawyers are in on
the big financial transactions, and in many cases they are
in on the formation of firms. Thirdly, I am also
cultivating the friendship of new accountants. Say, for
instance, a young accountant wants to break off from a
larger firm and start his own business. I'm more than
willing to lend him the money to get started, because he
can direct a lot of business my way. Even if a young
lawyer wants to borrow some money for a new car, I'm
most happy to because I believe in the future these
people will grow and by the time we're all 40 or 50 years
of age, there will be a lot of reciprocal sharing —
shooting business in each other's direction.*

"As a final note, it is of more than passing interest that this officer is able
not only to maintain good client relationships, which apparently have made
him a very productive lender, but at the same time he can keep an excellent
rapport with his colleagues, particularly his age peers. The young anti-
professional quoted at length earlier had the following to say. Coming from
him, it speaks well of the officer's interpersonal competence with clients and
with bank personnel alike.

*He's got a way of dealing with customers which is far
superior to mine. I might have the same level of credit
judgment, but when it comes to interpersonal relation-*

> *ships his style really stands out. Moreover, he has the complete confidence of the senior management, something which I don't and wish I had."*

Gerald Leader's work in this general area has cast some welcome light onto the problems inherent in a bank's customer and client dealings. It is clear that McMurry's cold and officious banker is one of a vanishing breed, but it is also clear that overly agressive individuals, in *their* manner of judging risks and taking responsibilities, can overdo the very drawbacks so deplored by McMurry. In the remainder of his thesis, Leader also examines those bank officers who are so dedicated to "service" that they are constantly worried that enough isn't being done and consequently work unneccesarily hard hours, complete with emotional fatigue, in a never-ending labor to improve service. Interestingly enough, where a "professional" is sometimes ineffective in the loan department, a service-oriented individual is often just as ineffective in the trust department. These individuals tend occasionally to get so wrapped up in "taking care" of the individuals whose money is in the trust that they neglect the fact that the trust has to provide some income for the bank as well.

Bearing in mind the popular image of the high-performance mutual fund manager, there is some reason to suspect that the reason that more discretionary savings are going into various funds, either for growth or for income, is due to the paternalistic attitudes evidenced by members of the trust department. They seem so concerned that the capital be conserved at all cost that they are as reluctant to make investment decisions as a "technical professional" is reluctant to make personality decisions with his loans. The result of this conservative style has caused an unfavorable comparison in which bank trust departments are often seen as a kind of mattress into which savings are stuffed for "a rainy day."

The publicity for the typical mutual funds, however, usually portrays the fund managers as a group of ruthless individuals who will work every trick in the trade to make sure that the funds entrusted to them provide the sort of earnings or growth which they have indicated as their goal. There is not a great deal of friendliness communicated, but there is the confidence that these people are interested in only one thing – the efficient handling of the funds entrusted to them. The respect, if not the warmth, engendered by this "technical" approach is often far more comforting to an individual than an overly protective style found among trust officers who are truly dedicated to "taking care of" the funds entrusted to them.

In summary, a bank is a place of business which is populated with many different types of people. Some bankers have chosen the bank as a refuge from the marketplace, the area in which they can ply the trade with a minimum of the sort of anxiety they encounter when having to rely on their intuition rather than their ratios. Nor do they have to come to terms with the human side of a business relationship. As Mr. Abel remarked, and as we have declared, the essence of good banking is good service, which often does not mean an efficient and meticulous manner when dealing with human beings. At the same time, the very "staidness" of the popular conception of a bank will at times prompt the original and creative businessman to launch a personal campaign to humanize his bank more for his own reasons than for the good of the bank.

It is hard to make any generalized classifications. As specialists in the social sciences, such meticulousness comes easy when preparing a study or structuring an interview session, but is often lacking in other areas of our lives. Understanding the nature of banking and the demands it places on an individual's skills and temperament is as helpful to the consumer psychologist as understanding the social sciences is helpful to a bank officer preparing to embark on an advertising or an image-building campaign. There is usually little to be lost in a thorough, honest analysis of the personality types associated with various trades and professions, and, in terms of understanding respect between people of different specialties, there is a great deal to be gained.

IV
SURVEY METHODS

Towards the last part of the nineteenth century, a few horseless carriages were sputtering and popping about the roads but there were no service stations. In most cases the owner would chug up to the general store in town and hope that it would have some gasoline. Gasoline didn't cost much, and there wasn't much demand; aside from some cleaning operations, its use was fairly limited because it was too volatile for most lamps. Those who became wealthy with oil wells did so through the sale of kerosene. If the pioneer motorist was lucky, the clerk would not keep him waiting too long for his three or four gallons. Then, after having ladled the smelly liquid out of the storage drum, the clerk would return to the regular cracker barrel customers.

In 1970 things move rapidly. Voices, ideas, letters, and information travel at the speed of light. The American public travels at a good clip as well, in hundreds of millions of automobiles. Shiny service stations dot the highways, strategically located to serve the most people. Attendants pump gas, clean windows, and occasionally vacuum your rugs. They are attentive and, if you are not careful, will often try to sell you everything from spark plugs to air cleaners before you leave the station. Additives compete against additives, and advertising carries the message into every home. The average customer is still mainly interested in a few gallons of gasoline, but there are now many customers and many other things which can be sold.

As the market for a commodity grows, business is not slow to offer it wherever it can be sold. Often modern business anticipates demands of the future and grows along with the demand so that there need be no catching up period. The gross national product is over a trillion dollars, reflecting the incredible expansion of commerce and markets in the last century. Never have so many people had so much money to spend. Money, the fuel of commerce and the driving force behind business, becomes less and less a substance and more and more a volatile force. And the institutions which deal in money, regulating its direction and flow, have more alternatives for action than ever before.

And yet banking still seems tied to the previous century in so far as the popular and the professional images of financial management are concerned. There are still huge steel vaults and locked boxes; imposing edifices and monumental facades seem to suggest that money, like gold, is a substance trundled from vault to vault under New York City. The bank has millions of new customers and hundreds of new services, and yet the shadow of the past lingers. The bank is an institution, the seat of professional ethics, and the prudent director of financial energy. The men who are called to the profession of banker are impressed with their responsibilities and their power. It is a seemly profession of gentlemen and paneled board rooms at the hub of business sophistication in the city. The tellers take it in and pay it out, while some customers receive personal service, when their requirements are deemed important enough.

An American working in an English travel agency, suggested one day that they might phone previous customers and alert them to some new tours. He was answered with a frosty glare; "Our customers know where we are," he was told, "and if they were satisfied, they will return when they wish to." This sense of splendid isolationism is fast disappearing from the American banking scene. The economy is moving too well to be able to wait for the customer. New banks spring up like mushrooms offering one enticement or another to lure savings and demand deposits. Like Alice's Red Queen, one has to move as fast as one can to stay even; to move ahead one must move twice as fast as that. But this is not to say that the new situation is a welcome change in style. Indeed, one might say that of all commercial businesses, banking has been dragged kicking and screaming into the marketplace to deal with merchants and common people. As the modern buildings rise and friendly faces appear on the television screens, one wonders whether they would, perhaps, be happier in the good old days when banking was a lofty profession and the town bank was an institution second only to the town hall. Do bankers really enjoy the rough and tumble of competition? Are they approaching market research unwillingly? Are advertising agencies friends or slick fellows who, unfortunately, must be employed to overstate and embellish the perfectly obvious, lest that "huckster bank" across the street attract all the newlyweds with their in-bank bridal fashion shows?

Do bankers want to be businessmen? They have no choice; they must be. Otherwise, there are lots of other places where the customer can place his surplus cash. Mutual funds send polished, attractive men from door to door, hardly as dignified as trust officers. Life insurance is beamed from magazine and television, and cars are bought with the help of time payments to the auto agency rather than a cash settlement and interest to the bank. Rather than face the sophisticated and highly intelligent loan officer, many people (some very affluent) perhaps feel a little below that station in life," borrow confidently from folks they trust at H. F. C.," where the interest is higher, but the personnel more approachable.

Yet the multi-million dollar operator of today was a small depositor thirty years ago. Was the bank careful of him then? Or has he never felt any attachment to the bank where he started? Is he now doing big business with another organization? The banks need people, all the people, big and small. And people are a lot more restless now than they were when there was one car in town and grandfather kept his savings in a sock. They have many more alternatives to consider when they wish to borrow, save, invest, or conserve, and banks are rising to this challenge. But how fast are they really adapting to the new business of being a service industry? Are they just racing to meet the demand, or are they looking ahead to prepare the modern techniques and applications which will enable them to be foremost in the potential or actual customer's mind? Will they be ready for the customer when he needs some new kind of financial service? Will they be there to welcome him, smart and smiling, into an association of mutual care and benefit?

These are questions which cannot be answered easily and which differ in scope from bank to bank. But there are methods and techniques which have been used for years in other industries to gain a good knowledge of the customer, to adapt business images and products to what the customer really wants. Banking isn't selling soap, but it is selling service; a service which is needed more and more through a relationship. There is no reason why the business of banking cannot benefit from the same technology and methodology which has enabled many other businesses to successfully adapt to a rapidly growing and changing market. The proper use of survey methods and in-depth interviewing is helping banks make the transitions demanded by our present social order. This chapter and the next one illustrate some of these approaches.

Marketing and sales approaches to banking are, in themselves, often considered new or even radical breaks with long standing tradition. As soon as a bank has decided to commit itself to a more aggressive business style, however, it becomes apparent that marketing in itself spans a number of separate areas. Each needs to be understood and taken into account before a comprehensive marketing strategy is decided upon. It would be very convenient if all businessmen were experts in all areas of business, but in this sphere there are few "Renaissance" men. It is an age of specialization, not so much because of the personal security felt in mastery of a certain craft, but because of a world in which the sum of human knowledge has grown so great that to become familiar with more than one area is often difficult, and mastery in several next to impossible. Lacking expertise in an area not your own does not mean, however, that you have to be uninformed to the extent of relying wholly on the suggestions of others when making decisions which impinge on that area.

A good loan officer must, for instance, often immerse himself in the workings of an industrial corporation which deals in products and methods almost completely unfamiliar to him. Soon, however, universal business traits become apparent. After a certain amount of the specialized vocabulary is learned, it becomes easy to deal with the manager of such a company, to be responsive to his needs and able to estimate the actual financial requirements of the firm. Banks are, in essence, a service industry, and it is usually easier for individuals in such industries to familiarize themselves with their customer's requirements rather than requiring manufacturers to become sensitive to the intricacies of finance which are so much more familiar to the professional banker.

Within the general field of marketing there are many strongly held opinions as to which single element is the most helpful in expanding the business of any firm. Some would argue for cleverly worded sales communications, others for more functional representation. Art experts usually are perfectly sure that an effective visual display is more effective than any wording at all. Advertising agencies are often of the opinion that good advertisements are the basis of successful marketing, while many customers would favor impressions given by pleasant and careful service. As social scientists, we feel that accurate knowledge concerning the wants and the needs of the consumer rank high on the list of information essential to a comprehensive and practical marketing program.

When we speak of "wants and needs" we are not making any assumptions as to how real these wants or needs are. In many cases a customer has been already prejudiced by any number of factors which might make him insensitive to logical or prudent appeals to his rational thinking. Wants and needs in a psychological context refers to the perceived wants or needs of any particular individual, no matter how far he may deviate from accepted norms. In most cases, however, there can be shown to be underlying similarities in the sorts of wants perceived by various segments of any given population. When these similarities are few enough, and one deals with a specific enough sub-group of consumers, it is not difficult to adapt advertising, slogans, artwork, and even service so that the firm employing these modes of communication will be seen as sensitive to, and concerned about, the desires it has perceived on the part of the consumer. If an executive of any given company elects to control his company's image so that it makes him feel comfortable, on the other hand, he will only appeal to that segment of the population which is similar to him in goals, values, and general life style. In the case of a bank that would mean a program that appealed to bankers, but might seem unresponsive to most of the bank's customers.

Here, then, is where the role of the consumer psychologist becomes important. He has been specifically trained in his field to be able to collect, record, and interpret data which can provide these necessary guidelines for a marketing program. Often, as in many specialized areas, the purchaser of such services is not at all familiar with his objectives, nor with the techniques one uses to obtain this wanted information. We hope to help explain the work of the consumer psychologist with a short discussion of the problems he faces, and the techniques used to obtain relevant and accurate information. We do not expect to turn any bankers into social scientists, but we hope that they will find it easier to deal with these specialists more effectively after learning more about their methodology and the reasons behind it.

Joseph Bachelder, in a talk given before the regional conference of Business Publications in October 1957, outlined some of the problems which confront any person who wishes to gauge consumer attitudes The problems haven't changed a bit in the last dozen years:

1. There are some people who know the reasons for their actions and will tell you.
2. There are some people who know the reasons for their actions but give you the wrong reasons.
3. There are those people who know the reasons for their actions but refuse to tell you.
4. There are those people who know the reasons for their actions and want to tell you, but have difficulty expressing themselves.
5. There are people who don't know the reasons for their actions but think they do and give you a reason.
6. There are those people who don't know the reasons but pretend that they do and lie to you.
7. There are those people who don't know why they acted as they did and refuse to say anything.
8. And there are even those who don't know why they acted as they did and can't even express their ignorance.

When a business customer asks for a loan, there are some ratios which a financial officer can depend on to give him the correct picture of just how this company is actually doing, despite anything the person requesting the loan may allege one way or the other. Likewise, there is the problem of asking just the right questions and phrasing them in such a manner that the person you are talking to understands what it is you wish to know. At times there is the more complex problem of trying to disguise your actual intent and still elicit meaningful information from the person you are talking with, just to make sure that his responses are spontaneous and honest if you are not convinced that he is sure of his ground. One has to be careful not to try so hard as to obtain a statement of strong feeling when the only time the individual really even considers the question is when an interviewer is talking to him. Finally, there is the problem of trying to determine just what a person really meant when he used certain words in response to your questions or in the course of an interview.

Many businessmen who have their doubts as to the value of opinion or attitude surveys are under the mistaken impression that all a consumer psychologist does is piece together a list of the most obvious questions, and then play darts with a sheet from the phone directory until he has called enough people and gotten enough answers to make up some important-sounding tables. This could be so if all respondents were of the first category — those who know the reasons for their actions and give you an accurate answer. This would be tantamount to the assumption that all people were equally prudent in their financial affairs and always acted in the most logical and rational manner when allocating borrowed capital. And as any banker will tell you, it would be a far easier world for him if such were the case. As it is, specialists are needed for help in interpreting data and information correctly.

There have been many methods used in the attempt to obtain accurate data. At one time it was thought (and still is in some advertising agencies) that the accuracy of a poll increased as the number of respondents increased. This particular school of thought was substantially discredited in 1936 when the *Literary Digest* concluded from a poll of seven million people, the largest poll ever taken, that Franklin D. Roosevelt would lose his bid for a second term. By control, the Gallup and Roper polls, making use of a system which tried to select representative samples from all walks of life, interviewed a small fraction of the population and accurately predicted a Democratic victory. Variations of this method of selective sampling are used today to make the election night forecasts, which often seem to have an uncanny ability to predict results within a few percentage points when only a small number of votes are actually in. *It is most important to be able to select your respondents as carefully as you select your questions.*

Next there is the problem of causing an artificial situation which of itself causes the respondent to answer questions or discuss a topic in a manner unlike his normal, unprompted way. No matter how fair-minded an individual, when confronted by a question or a questioner he will often react with an answer demonstrative of the way he thinks he ought to respond, when he might in reality feel quite differently about the situation. This means that the psychologist must take into account any possible distortion that his mere presence may have induced in the information he is able to collect. These distortions can be of any nature. They may, for instance, depend on whether the individual is highly opinionated and wants an audience, or is submissive and fears correction by others if his opinions are rejected by his group.

One of the more ingenious attempts to eliminate this sort of error entirely was recently carried out by two psychologists from Harvard University. Rather than question inhabitants of several small towns as to their political leanings, they addressed several thousand envelopes. Half were addressed to a well known right-wing organization, while the rest were addressed to a similarly well known left-wing group. In both cases the letter inside was an innocuous message of greeting to a friend. The letters were then stamped, sealed and dropped in a random pattern from a low flying plane during several passes over the towns they were investigating. Their reasoning was that a person of conservative views might not even mail what he took to be a mislaid, stamped letter if it were addressed to a group whose opinions he was at odds with. The number of liberal individuals in the town would have a similar effect on the number of right-wing letters mailed. The addressees, of course, actually directed the letters back to the psychologists who were then able to count up the number of letters of each type mailed and make an estimate of the political nature of the town without ever talking to a single person. This experiment eliminated one form of distortion, but worked only by giving the average person the choice of helping an organization which he would probably have very strong feelings about. It is unlikely that the average bank customer would object to mailing a stamped, addressed envelope to a bank he did not like, no matter how intense his feelings might be.

It is sometimes easier to test responses to a particular product or advertisement than it is to assess feeling about certain sorts of businesses or services. This task of trying to pin down a respondent to some clear opinions becomes even more difficult if we do not wish him to know that we are, say, running a survey on a certain bank's charge-card plan. There are accepted psychological tests, such as the Thematic Apperception Test (or TAT) in which the subject is asked to describe in his own words what is happening in a picture whose theme is actually open to many interpretations. By means of such a test, we can get a good idea of what sort of a person is being interviewed, but it will not give us any solid opinions. The ideal survey might well include a test such as this for each respondent before any pertinent questions were brought up, just to have a means of assessing what sort of person was answering the questions. A procedure such as this, however ideal, would be both too time consuming and too intricate to be within the practical financial limits of any consumer survey. Usually the psychologist has to rely on his own training to make these assessments, judging, for example, the manner in which the respondent answered certain questions, or the words he chose in his conversation about a topic.

At the other end of the spectrum, there is the excessively simplistic technique used by some opinion-polling organizations. These simply telephone a number of people in an essentially random manner and record the answers to a certain number of questions. Another slant is to give the respondent a series of objects, or situations, or ideas and have him rank them in some order. This sort of opinion poll is often seen in the popular press because it is relatively easy to get the sort of responses which will tally into what appears to be a conclusive report on likes or dislikes. The first method assumes that all respondents will answer accurately and that they are concerned about the subject being investigated, the second does not even take into account ideas that the respondent himself may have. When a housewife is asked to rate "Fluffo, Bluffo and Muffo" in order of preference, the results may indeed indicate that 43% of housewives rated Bluffo over Muffo. In actuality, if the interviewer had asked "What do you prefer to use on your dishes," he might well have found that Mrs. Housewife preferred Bluffo to Muffo, but that she liked Blastoff even better and used it almost constantly. It is sometimes difficult for the social scientist to conduct a survey which he feels is both conclusive and accurate while keeping within the budgetary requirements of the firm retaining his services.

When we do an attitude and opinion survey, we employ a combination of techniques which deliver fairly sure results without predisposing the respondent. If the survey is to be fairly large and general in nature, such as gauging prevalent feelings among commercial bank customers towards a particular bank's expansion program, we usually conduct the study in three separate steps.

The first stage is to carry out highly unstructured group or personal interviews of selected individuals who represent, as a sample, the group at whom we are directing the study. This means that there is some time devoted in the very beginning to classifying a population, such as business customers, into representative segments. Usually between fifty and a hundred individuals are chosen, and the first interviews may take as long as two or three hours. The interviews are, at this point, open-ended, which is to say that instead of being prepared with specific questions we simply introduce a topic and encourage the subject to speak his own mind on the whole area. We often employ a tape recorder at this stage to catch any comment which might pertain to the specific questions we will eventually be asking. Sometimes we assemble a group of five to ten individuals at one time, in comfortable surroundings, since the presence of similar people often acts as an encouragement to share one's feelings or prompts a group member to air his opinions to see the sort of response he receives. No matter which approach is used, we always start in this undirected manner, asking the respondent to give us his whole range of feelings and opinions in a general area.

After some time of keeping the conversation going, and when we feel that the respondent has said all he would under a more or less spontaneous setting, we "focus-in" an attempt to elicit more information by means of more specific questions. This might be by asking a respondent to amplify on some statements already made, or it might take the form of several psychological "games". One such game consists of our beginning a sentence and having the respondent finish it in his own words. We might say "The president of a bank should . . . ." and let the respondent say what he thinks a bank president should be or do, how he should appear, or anything else he might come up with. Although some of these sentences are designed to lessen the emphasis on the points we are seriously trying to study, the majority of them are so worded as to prompt specific attitudinal information. Often we will experiment with word association, giving the respondent a word, such as "trust department," and having him respond with the first adjective which comes into his head. Other times we will prepare in advance a list of fifty or more adjectives and ask him to select any one or number of them which would more or less correspond with his feelings towards an object, a service, or a situation.

When we have completed these fifty to a hundred interviews in this manner, we go over the data we have gathered with an eye towards detecting any sort of patterns which seem to be similar from person to person or within a segment. Often many individuals will, quite independently, select the same descriptive words to describe their attitudes towards something we have brought up in the interview. From this sort of information, we can learn what areas mean a lot to which sorts of people and where opinions seem the most diverse.

When the data has been thoroughly studied and classified, we draw up a preliminary projective questionnaire which, based on the information already received, would elicit the sort of answers which we could code and classify more easily. By using this technique, we are using the respondents themselves to design a series of questions which will tend to give us the most useful information in the most efficient manner.

The second stage is quite similar to the first and really serves as a test for the questionnaires and interview topics we chose after studying the results of the first interviews. Again, fifty to one hundred representative individuals are selected and interviewed, only this time in a less open-ended manner and for a shorter period of time. From the results of these interviews, we can modify or augment certain portions of the questionnaires to make them even more selective. As usual, the data from this second stage is also recorded and coded for later computer tabulation.

Our questionnaires are now honed to a fine degree of accuracy. They are both appropriate in tone for our population and suitable for gathering the most information in the least amount of time. Then we embark on the third stage, which can be as large a sample as desired. Since we do not have to engage in long interviews in this third stage, we can cover a great many people in far less time and still come up with data which is direct and pertinent. Sometimes we conduct three to five hundred short interviews using the structured questionnaire. At times it is possible to do much of the questioning over the telephone. At any rate, with the questionnaire matched specifically to the people we are studying, this last stage does not have to be conducted by trained psychologists — a factor of some importance, given a limited budget.

When all the interviewing has been completed, we classify and code the answers onto punch cards for computer analysis. This is not difficult when one has kept this final step in mind from the beginning and has written the questionnaires in such a way that the information obtained can be easily so transferred. After the normal summing and averaging operations, we can program for more specific information by cross-tabulating the data. We could, for instance, cross-tab "age forty to fifty" with the adjective "protective" when used with "bank officer". In a matter of seconds, the computer will speed through literally months of interviews and print out that "23.7% of those over forty but under fifty see bank officers as "protective". This is the sort of work which could be extremely tedious and time consuming were it not for the speed of the modern digital computer. If we wished to split hairs, we could come up with fascinating information such as "5.8% of retail electric appliance dealers who have two children and a dog use more than one bank". This would not be very helpful, but one can see what this sort of programming can do if used with a structured questionnaire. It could be very helpful to know, say, what percentage of corporations founded after 1950 use which services of which bank.

When all the study and tabulation is completed, we transfer the data onto tables (sometimes more than a hundred pages) and write up a general summary. If there have been specific areas under scrutiny, we try to interpret the results with an eye towards meaningful suggestions for action by management. Our methods would not be appropriate for some other sorts of surveys, especially ones which attempted to assess a very large population's feelings about one or two specific points. For an accurate and fairly complete rendering of attitudes and opinions of a specific group of consumers towards a range of services, it seems to be one of the best combinations of techniques in use today and is used by many organizations conducting this sort of study.

When a bank is thinking of having a consumer survey done, it may be well to determine first, with the help of a research firm experienced in banking, what information you wish to get. This will make the task of the psychologist a lot easier than a general description of many areas you would like to know about. After a study team has been told what the bank wants to know, the polling organization should be asked to explain their techniques so that the bank understands thoroughly what they are doing and how they are doing it. Despite a lot of complicated scientific jargon which can be used in describing the parameters of the representive samples, the mean scale deviations from the accepted norm, optimum sample sizes and theories of statistical analysis (with corresponding numerical and algebraic formulas), there is actually very little that cannot be explained in simple terms to a layman's complete satisfaction.

Be sure to remember those eight categories of answers which interviewers are likely to receive, and be confident in your own mind that the organization or individual that you retain has the expertise not to just count heads or ask questions which "seem" helpful. There are too many variables in this area to risk "rule of thumb" guesses in the early stages.

V

PRELIMINARY IN-DEPTH INTERVIEWING

The first two stages of an attitude or opinion survey, as we have noted, are the intensive, in-depth interviews which pave the way for a meaningful questionnaire composed of relevant questions to be used in the hundreds of shorter interviews which comprise much of the last stage. In this chapter we shall look more closely at the techniques used and some of the responses elicited during these preliminary sessions.

When compared to the later stages of the attitude survey, the first stages are more instructive and, to a large extent, more interesting than tabulating the responses to the final sets of questions. Interpreting open-ended interviews is far more time-consuming, but it is the challenging task of the psychologist to glean from hundreds of statements and snatches of conversation the basic motivations and true feelings of his respondents. Asking questions isn't enough; one must play both watchdog and detective, alert to undercurrents of feelings which are not actually articulated and ready to alter the thrust of the conversation to help a respondent clarify his own feelings and opinions without seeming to probe or prompt.

Of the two types of preliminary interviews, the group sessions are more interesting to the outside observer since the interplay of conversation between relaxed individuals can often bring out hidden feelings and attitudes more readily than a single session between a respondent and the psychologist. Transcripts of the single interviews, however, often point up the fact that relatively random conversation, when put into print, seems to be far more directive and easily interpreted than it might have first seemed. This is why the psychologist, if he is not recording the conversations during a preliminary interview, must take copious, verbatim transcripts which can later be typed into a form for review and study. Although the psychologist must be sensitive enough to ad-lib his questions during the actual course of the conversation, the end result of allowing an individual to come to his own conclusions off the cuff often results in some surprisingly clear indications of how the respondent actually is biased, no matter how fair-minded he may consider himself. The following accounts of three interviews show the impact of careful, professional interviewing. The results are so clear that it is not even necessary to be a psychologist to divine the motivations and feelings of an individual who thinks that he is just rambling on about a subject.

The first transcript reveals an individual who, although affable and relaxed, obviously harbors some deep-seated misgivings about banks in general. What makes this important is that he is the comptroller of the regional offices of a major U. S. manufacturing company. He loves his work and, in spite of the occasional frustrations involved in it, would not want to work in any other area. He was in his mid-fifties at the time of the interview, married, and had a son in college. He spoke easily, and was very definite in his opinions. He emphasized his points with mild profanity from time to time.

"I have dealt with banks most of my life, and personally I think they stink. I have always felt that they don't even like to see you coming in. Most banks act as though they are doing you a favor to accept your business. It seems as if they care very little about the people they are supposed to serve. Banks have impressed me as wanting and demanding a great deal from their clients and being willing to give very little in return. The interest that they give you on your money is low, while the interest that they charge on loans is high in comparison. They charge you for every little service they render and if you request some little special service, they treat you like a dog or a criminal. *Frankly I have always felt uncomfortable in banks.* I object to the haughty, superior manner with which they treat you, and if you make some honest mistake in dealing with them, they try to make you feel as if you're stupid and uncooperative. *I have always felt* that banks are high-handed and critical. *Sometimes they remind me of the way strict parents act toward children.* They try to give you the feeling that because they control so much money they are all-powerful.

"Commercial banks are the worst. They are cold, unfriendly and not at all helpful. They are now tending to curtail the services they offer and charge for every little thing they do. The commercial bank is most unfair in the way it serves its clients. If you're a big account, they treat you fairly well. If you're a small account, they don't care much about you."

At this point the respondent compared the manner in which his commercial bank treated him as a comptroller of a large corporation with the power to withdraw a large account, to the way in which he felt he was treated at the bank in which he did his personal banking and had only a small account. He felt that his small account resulted in an uncaring and uncooperative attitude toward him by that bank.

"The relationship between a businessman and a bank should be a personalized and individual one, with a mutual understanding of each other's requirements and problems. There should be a real friendliness and respect. The relationship under present conditions is too cold and impersonal. Commercial banks could be improved if the bank managers would take the time to try and understand the psychology of people. Then they would realize that customers need recognition and the personal touch. The bank manager has much to do with the manner in which a bank is run. Commercial banks could be improved by offering more individualized services, by being more lenient in collateral requirements for loans, and by being more flexible in the interpretation of existing regulations. I think that commercial banks could be greatly improved by having representatives of the bank make regular personal calls upon clients at their offices to discuss their problems and try to work out ways to serve them better. These personal interviews could be conducted about every two months.

"My own experiences with banks have not been particularly pleasant. They are too cold and formal. They never make a friendly gesture. The only time they ever contact you is when something is wrong. If other business acted the way banks do, it wouldn't last six months. Its customers would leave it flat. I have never changed banks, but have stayed with the same ones. This doesn't mean that I am satisfied with them. There have been times when I have been very angry with banks, but I have always calmed down and never did or said anything. *I guess most people are, deep down, a little afraid of banks.* I believe that people select a commercial bank on a statistical basis. That is, they select a bank which gives the impression of *stability and efficiency.* I personally, however, would select a bank that is friendly and informal like a small town savings bank. I have never had any particularly pleasant experiences with commercial banks. As a business executive, I have not had any really unpleasant experiences with commercial banks because they respected the size of the corporation which I represented. However, as a private individual, I have had several unpleasant experiences. On only two occasions in my life have I mistakenly overdrawn my checking account, but the bank was very irate and acted as if I were a criminal. They were most impatient concerning the time allowed to cover the deficiency in funds. Another time I made an error in making out a deposit form which had been recently changed. Instead of helping me to correct it, the teller sent me away from the window twice until I had gotten the correct form completed. The teller was nasty and *treated me like a naughty child.*

"Most business use more than one commercial bank because they don't want to put all their eggs in one basket. It's a good idea not to have people in one bank know all your business. *Bankers are generally pretty curious and nosey people. The less they know about one's total financial picture, the better.* Sometimes bankers talk more than they should in their off-hand conversations. People choose one particular commercial bank because they are impressed with its size and power. I personally would select a commercial bank if I felt that it would give individualized attention to my financial problems."

In response to sentence — completion questions, the respondent gave these examples of his feelings:

1. When I was a kid, I felt that banks were — a place to go to deposit your money.
2. Compared to trust companies, commercial banks — do not render as personalized a service.
3. Bankers probably feel — that I am looking for something for nothing.
4. Most executives feel that commercial banks — are cold and impersonal.
5. Most bankers see their customers as — individuals who are looking for services that they are not willing to pay for.
6. The ideal ads for a commercial bank should — indicate friendliness and stability.

In looking back upon this interview we can come to some fairly definite conclusions about how this individual feels about banks. Bearing in mind that this particular interview is not recent one could say that this man's views were more common then than they are today. One thing does seem to stand out, however; while he is castigating the banks with which he does his business, he is at the same time making it fairly obvious that his bias is almost entirely of his own making. It would not take a Freudian psychiatrist to note the several times that he equates the bank with a stern father, and himself with the naughty child.

Most bank officers would probably react with something like "If he has a problem, or is dissatisfied, why doesn't he say something about it? We'd be more than glad to help him out." This is precisely why a psychologist is a helpful adjunct to a bank marketing program. Somewhat like a priest or a doctor, a psychologist is more usually seen as an unbiased and even sympathetic person with whom one can be honest without fear of retribution. This respondent has already built up such negative attitudes towards banks that he sees bankers as innately unfriendly. He would be most unlikely to come to a banker with a problem since he feels already that the banker has a negative attitude towards him. This feeling seems to date back many years. He says that he has *always* felt uncomfortable with banks. He has never given the banker a chance and probably never will, unless the banker goes more than halfway to assure him of the bank's friendliness and concern. This fantasy of being the object of negative feelings eventually results in his own mistrust of banks. In one sentence, he says that bankers should be more lenient about their collateral requirements, and shortly later he criticizes bankers for being nosey and advises the interviewer not to tell a banker the true financial picture. This is obviously inconsistent. What banker in his right mind would be lenient with an individual who was trying to be evasive about his company's financial situation? The only defense this man seems to have is the size of his company's account, which, he feels, is the only reason he isn't worked over every time he walks into a bank.

The value of this sort of an interview is quite clear. Given the opportunity to speak freely, a respected executive and financial officer of a major manufacturing concern, *the one individual who would probably have the most contact with the company's bank, turns out to be highly irrational about commercial banks.* This is precisely why social scientists speak of perceived needs as against actual needs. This man perceives banks as unfriendly, although they are not so. He needs to be reassured constantly that banks *are* friendly; if this relatively powerful financial figure can be scared by a mere teller into feeling like a naughty child, he needs powerful reassurance to overcome this fear. A bank not only has to exhibit friendly actions, but *it also has to create the image of friendliness.*

Since this man's negative feelings are based on an unrealistic image of bankers, he could have equally positive feelings for an equally unrealistic image. We are not suggesting that banks attempt to portray themselves dishonestly. But by stressing concern and attention, even if the officers know that this sort of attention to multitudes of retail customers would be difficult, the bank can prompt the formation of positive attitudes in current and prospective customers. It is highly unlikely that a customer would go so far as to greet the head financial officer of the bank with a cordial "Hi Fred, how's the wife!" But if he had a problem, he would not be afraid to go to that officer and seek the help which most bank officers are very willing to offer. If the comptroller of a major, multi-million dollar company is nervous about banks, one can imagine how unwilling a private citizen with only a few hundred dollars on deposit would be to discuss his financial plans and needs openly with a bank official.

The next interview shows another picture. The same informal setting existed in this respondent's office, and the same questions were asked. He was also in his mid fifties, and was the treasurer of an established, fairly large retailing establishment.

"Banks remind me of money, [shrugs] a way of payment of bills . . an easier way of taking care of obligations than using cash. [commercial banks?] Here, I think of substantial citizens of the community. [Friendly?] I have a warm feeling for banks. [When you were younger?] I was more hesitant than today in dealing with them . . . a little nervous. If you wanted to borrow, you had to feel you had a right to go in. Now I just call up and it's a normal business transaction. Banks look pretty pretentious. With the X bank, for instance, you might think that you're too small to be considered. Now I know they love to see you come.

"[Ideal commercial banks?] Should be sound, reputable; it is good to know some of the officers, to have confidence in them. Employees and contact people should be friendly and be known as good citizens. You want to feel that you have confidence in their experience. Bankers should know more about what you want than you do. They should give counsel and advice. If I were going into business and needed financing, I would go there for advice. Bankers should be more scrupulous than other businessmen, above reproach in their living habits, less shrewd in their dealings than some business people have to be. [Women in banking?] You would expect to have women officers to handle female customers. [Relationship of banker to business-men?] My relationship would be like that with any other businessman . . . a first name proposition, socially friendly, might play golf together. It would be proper for the banker to do almost anything any businessman would. However, you have more confidence in what the banker tells you as advisor and consultant. In other relationships, like buyer and seller, there is more a stretch in the facts. You don't expect any stretch in bank salesmanship; they must be above reproach. Our banks continually make friendly calls . . . 'hope you'll remember us' or 'never hesitate to call if you need us.' I would give them as much time as any salesman. They should send literature on what the bank is and how strong it is. I would rather see TV ads for banks than those hammering aspirin. Bank ads are a higher type, a more quiet type that don't disturb you. They tell you that they're friendly, that you're welcome.

"[Pleasant experience with banks?] Bigger the bank, more pleasant the experience. When you're in a tight squeeze, they're stronger and can take risks more easily. Today I walk into Bank X freely. When I was younger, I was afraid of Bank X because of its bigness; it made me feel small and unimportant. I won't name the bank that refused us a loan. They thought it was too big a risk; we knew that it posed a troublesome problem for them. [Selection of a bank?] The location is important, but more important is to know some particular person at the bank. Status of the bank financially would have bearing on a larger account. X bank is very high in my mind, one of the best banks in town to do business with. Down to earth, friendly officers, you wouldn't think that they were a big bank the way they treat you. I think of them as an organization, to call up about anything."

1. When I was a kid I felt banks were — institutions, monuments on Main Street.
2. Compared to trust companies, commercial banks are — similar except for their charter.
3. Bankers probably feel — that I am a capable businessman.
4. Most executives feel that commercial banks are — well-run and useful.
5. Most bankers see their customers — frequently.
6. The ideal ads for a commercial bank would be — direct mail.

This sort of a customer is the type that most banks are happy to have and eager to retain. It is interesting to note, however, that the respondent was, at one time, also nervous and hesitant about making use of a bank. One or two good experiences changed him from a person with neutral or negative feelings into an individual with a high regard for banks. And, it appears, these were instances in which he felt that the banks were outgoing and helpful. It should be stressed, however, that it looks as if this man was able to discover the helpfulness of banks after he had been to them with his problems and needs, and found out, probably to his surprise and delight, that they could be concerned and helpful. This, again, is not a very accurate picture. We have a person who, having been approved by an institution which he had qualms about, changed his attitudes distinctly. He switched from one side to another once he felt that a large and potentially unfriendly institution was indeed reasonable and helpful. We again are face to face with the problem: *unless a person actually goes to banks to discover how helpful they can be, he will probably remain nervous and even possibly antagonistic towards them.*

Our third respondent was a financial executive of a large office equipment manufacturer. Under identical conditions, he had this to say about banks:

"[How do you feel about banks?] I feel that we would be in terrible shape without them. They provide everyone with a sense of security. The most important thing in a bank is the bankers. They should be of high caliber. One of the things that is missing in banks is generosity. [What do you mean by generosity?] Not mean or prejudiced. Another thing, the people handling the public have not reached the desired educational level . . . and they should be sales-minded. People make an organization, not machines. [What personality would be best?] One that enjoys people. It is true that an elevator boy meets more people than any executive, but this meeting of people is a bit different for a banker. [Please explain?] Well, it is like a doctor having a bedside manner. Bankers need a sympathetic manner. [Just what is a good manner?]

They need to be good listeners. The bankers also need good appearance and conservative habits. [What do you call conservative?] Being conservative in dress — white shirt, pressed suit and a shine on the shoes. The problem of drinking — social drinking, not to be hanging around cheap bars — and not to be around the race track. Businessmen should feel that they can safely confide in a banker. [How personal can they get?] If it is a good banker and a good businessman, then it is O. K. for them to get personal. Anyway, a banker and a good businessman both choose their friends with discretion.

"[How do people select a bank] By the special services. I know of a large account that was gotten through the wives at a bridge party. [How did you decide to use the bank you now have?] The aggressive guy gets your business. When I arrived here from New York, three bankers came up to see me. They were all the same. I could have flipped a coin. [How did you select the bank that you did?] One of them took a greater interest. [pause] Being new in town, he offered to help me get located, said that he would see that checks would always be cashed — that sort of thing, personal services."

1. When I was a kid, I thought that banks were — a place to put money.
2. Compared to trust companies, commercial banks are — a depositary of funds.
3. Banks probably feel that I — might be a good depositor.
4. Most executives feel — that commercial banks are essential to growth of business.
5. Most bankers see their customers — as customers.
6. The commercial bank ads I like best — are conservative.
7. When I enter a bank, I feel — at home.

This individual seemed, from a banker's point of view, probably the most fair-minded of all. He neither felt intimidated by banks, nor was he very favorably excited by them. He saw them, in a word, as businesses. If his answers to these questions had been elicited on a phoned questionnaire, a banker could point with pride and say: "Well, there are still some sensible businessmen around this city." From a psychological point of view, however, that would have to be classified as an inaccurate interpretation. We didn't mention one factor which came up in the course of the conversation: history and childhood experiences with banks. "That's not a fair question." [Why?] Well, I was raised and born in the banking business. My father was the president of a bank."

It seems as if the opinions which most bankers would judge as being most accurate come from bankers themselves, or those closely associated with banking. No matter how logical or fair bankers see themselves to be, this sort of informal, conversational in-depth interview was able to yield information which enabled us to realize that to most people banks were, or at least had been, formidable institutions that stood in judgment. If you felt that you were not up to par in their eyes, you tended to be antagonistic. If you felt that you had passed muster, on the other hand, you would tend to bask in this approval and feel very comfortable about banks. Very rarely was there an even-minded approach to the business of banking such as was displayed by the third respondent.

By means of such long, informal interviews, the social scientist can gain a great deal of essential information which is of utmost importance in designing an accurate set of questions for a larger group of interviews. Occasionally, we conduct group interviews in which a selected number of executives are invited for dinner at a hotel and afterwards simply have an informal discussion of the selected topic. As we have noted in the previous chapter, this sort of atmosphere of relaxation and informality can be helpful by enabling the respondents to clarify their own feelings in discussion with others. Often they can begin to get down beneath the surface to discover just how they formed their attitudes towards various institutions. When conducting this sort of an interviewing session, we generally tape-record (even video) the whole discussion and transcribe it later to investigate feelings and motivations which would never have been apparent from a simple telephone interview or a short meeting with a prepared questionnaire.

Eventually, through trial and error, and after a good deal of time in thoughtful analysis, a conclusive and meaningful interview form can be prepared by asking the right questions in the right manner. It can elicit from large numbers of people the sorts of responses which generate a highly accurate attitude profile of a large number of people.

In summary, the in-depth interviews indicate the best areas to study in a larger survey. These questions are formulated in two ways: open ended questions to allow spontaneous reactions and structured attitude scales that yield agree or disagree type responses. Usually, the interview form is, as mentioned above, tested on at least fifty people before its use on a large population. In doing a study, *we are forming hypotheses and predictions* about a bank and its retail or business public, about the competition, about advertising, calling officers, the checking account market, and other areas of client interest. These hypotheses are constantly refined and in our analysis of the data we draw conclusions about each of these problems.

The composition of the final sample is selected in terms of our specific objectives in a given study. The analysis is made qualitatively and through the use of computer techniques. Suggestions for action are developed from the results of the study, from our previous experience in bank studies and in psychology, and from our knowledge of the social contexts and practical realities faced by the client. The total procedure is a mixture of science and art in which we attempt, by virtue of our training, to make our work scientific yet practical, precise yet somewhat subjective. It must be clear enough for a fact-oriented bank to accept the approach of psychology, which is more "feeling-oriented" than the usual world in which bankers deal. Therefore, in order to optimize our effectiveness, we stress the communication of findings, the interchange between client and researcher, and the contact between advertising agency and all levels of the bank's staff.

VI

INCREASING THE EFFECTIVENESS OF
BANK ADVERTISING

Quite recently we were called in on a consulting basis to help a commercial bank in its use of newspaper advertisements. The bank was a medium-large one in a medium-sized city within the New York-Philadelphia corridor. It's customers included both local industries and a sizable retail trade which ranged beyond the immediate area.

Newspaper advertisements are a fundamental tool for transmitting information from commercial banks to their customers. Usually, because of the superior ability of personalities to effectively communicate ideas by means of television, newspaper advertising does not get its share of the credit. In 1961 a research firm did a study of nearly seven thousand men and women, classified by age and income groups in several geographic areas. The aim of the survey was to determine the attitudes of the public towards five major communication media. The results of this study, especially when compared with others done earlier in the same area, are very informative.

Apparently, television was at the height of its credibility around 1957. The over-use of hard-sell messages and the publicity surrounding the rigged quiz shows greatly affected this credibility during the next five years. By the early sixties, when banks were beginning to awaken to the possibilities of this medium, favorable associations connected with television had deteriorated. These associations began to rise again, but television was still considered a medium to be taken with a grain of salt. Words such as "insincere" and "deceptive" continued to appear in interviews. Studies done at that time showed conclusively that print advertising was considered more accurate than television, since many people continued to identify television[1] primarily as an entertainment medium. This being the case, they looked upon television commercials as the "price of admission," a disturbance to be tolerated. A

1. However the Institute for Consumer Psychology finds television the best remembered advertising medium.

large majority of those included in the study considered newspaper advertising "less entertaining" but more sincere — not as interesting, but "more reliable".

Research has indicated that much advertising fails because it does not succeed in its primary objective, which is to "identify, distinguish, and inform." A successful advertisement must accomplish all of these things. In addition, it hopefully must motivate the consumer into some course of action, and it usually has to accomplish these goals at home or when the consumer is relaxed.

It becomes easy to see how good newspaper advertising can be of great benefit to banking institutions. Not only is the medium one which seems to be quite highly trusted, but the exposure is apt to be at a-time of relaxation: over the morning coffee, commuting to one's place of business, or when relaxing after lunch or dinner. Indeed, when one considers the readership of newspapers, one sees that this form of advertising is far more selective when it comes to bringing a message to a prospective large account holder. Very few influential businessmen read less than one newspaper a day, and often several more, while their television viewing is considerably below the national average.

We proceeded in the project by first reviewing recent newspaper advertising for the bank involved and for the other banks which advertised in the major city newspaper. The ads varied a great deal in their effectiveness and were not easy to classify as a group since many advertisements were from banks in other large metropolitan areas which had advertising resources well beyond our bank. In looking at all these advertisements, including our bank's, several questions came to mind. Do people remember bank advertisements after they see them? How many people do? And, most significantly, are these people customers or non-customers of the respective banks?

This last consideration is most important because research has strongly indicated that mass communication is generally more likely to reinforce the existing opinions of its audience than it is to change these opinions. Minor attitude change is more likely than any dramatic conversion, but even this is rare. This is partly because the message is mediated by several factors quite outside the realm of the advertisement itself. Most people tend to expose themselves selectively to communications which are in accord with their existing views. Furthermore, they retain such messages better. Again, those who have a personal interest in the item being advertised are more likely to remark on it to other people who are likely to be interested. Finally, many people seem to be far more responsive to those whom they regard as "opinion leaders" than they are to printed communications from an abstract company. As a matter of fact, data has been studied which indicates that personal influence is as much as seven times more effective than newspaper or magazine advertising in persuading some individuals to switch their brands or accounts. Most of the reaction to a good bank advertisement would be reinforcement to those already being served by the bank, although, hopefully, the ad might prompt some "opinion leaders" to literally become so reinforced that they would start mentioning the bank to their associates. We had to ask ourselves to what extent we could locate data which would tell us whether this was happening. We needed information to see if people, prompted by the advertisements, were calling the bank, visiting the bank to open an account or transact other business, or were telling others about what they saw in the ad.

Since this particular assignment was, for use, consultative and not an in-depth study, we were not able to undertake the sort of survey which might have revealed the answers in a direct manner. On the other hand, after carefully reviewing the material at hand, it was possible to offer comments and suggestions.

The first advertisement we studied promoted savings accounts. Like many similar ads, it had a list of advantages, numbered along one side of the page. Since it consisted for the most part of printed copy, we felt there was some question as to how many people would actually commit themselves to reading the whole message, and how much of the message had to be read for the message to actually come across.

The second ad heralded the opening of a new branch, and could have been improved considerably. Here was an excellent opportunity to emphasize newness and the capacity of the bank to grow with the times, as well as its ability to prepare for future growth. The bank could have easily and truthfully been presented as a public-oriented, cooperative sort of institution. Instead, the ad simply reported the new office in a way which did not seem very out of the ordinary.

Other ads that we saw made more use of photography. People invariably like pictures unless they are looking for extremely dependable information. This does not mean that ads utilizing photographs will give any sense of undependability, for the sorts of information we refer to here are serious announcements such as obituaries, stock reports, and public records. This is not pleasurable information, but it may be something one feels one has to know, and so one is willing to endure the lack of humanizing decoration in order to get the information needed as quickly and as efficiently as possible. In all other forms of communication, however, the broader the visual appeal, the more receptive the audience. With banks, this can be a rather touchy subject, since many bank officers feel that a serious approach is the proper one to promote an image of security. The fact is that banks are already security symbols; unless a bank is in an old house trailer and is subject to several robberies each year, the average customer already thinks of it as a safe, secure, and dependable fortress full of prudent men. But these men may not be viewed as the most pleasant with whom to do business. The task, therefore, is to promote the fact that of all the secure, dependable, and prudent banks, your bank is by far the nicest and most helpful.

Other ads for the bank studied had more use of photography. One which seemed particularly effective promoted a Christmas Club, and it included a picture of a man and an attractive girl. No matter what the copy, this ad would probably catch the eye and hold it for a longer time than would those advertisements based on copy alone.

After consulting with the bank's public relations and advertising coordinator, we developed some new ideas concerning the sorts of advertising which could gain more readership, more recall, and more impact. The first point we stressed was that to be more effective the ads would have to incorporate more emotional appeal. Rather than simply being factual, we felt that they should be distinctive and attention-getting. It was recommended, therefore, that the bank try to create advertisements which would develop personal involvement as well as a direct theme and appeal. A further suggestion was that the bank develop means through which their advertising might contain both elements of realism as well as an appeal to the reader's fantasy and his ability to imagine the sort of bank he wishes his bank to be.

The first series of advertisements that the management had developed made use of the theme "Friends of Yours Save at Bank X." The three newspaper ads using this copy made use of drawings at the top of the ad and photographs at the bottom. In two cases, the drawings were of different types of houses. The third contained pictures of appliances and sporting equipment. The photographs were, in all three cases, of employees of the bank. After studying these three, we decided that there would be more involvement if people were shown not only in at the bottom of the ad, but also in the main drawing or photograph. We felt that having people in the main part of the ad would probably attract more attention than would more objects. The inclusion of people would make it easier for the viewer to project himself into the ad and thus identify with the message.

After this initial conference, the bank switched to a slightly changed copy appeal of "Friends you know work at bank X." This seemed much better, as it was an implied testimonial and a distinctive, easy to remember theme. It was believable as well, since it included pictures of those working at the bank. It was a humanizing theme, one which viewers could identify with since it created the impression that those associated with the bank enjoyed fun and "the good life," a life which was made easier by the service of a bank that shared the goals of its customers.

There was no question in our minds that this type of approach was more credible and appealing than the previous one. The new advertisement carried two messages at once, since it was also an appeal for new and badly-needed employees. Since the photographs at the bottom included people of diverse racial and ethnic backgrounds, the appeal was particularly apt for a bank in a metropolitan area. These photographs also indicated the bank's concern for minority groups.

Four specific advertisements were then developed. One showed drawings of a family at the Lincoln Memorial. This ad presented the bank as the agent which was instrumental in helping a family enjoy its trip. Although the copy did not make specific references to any particular service, the implication was that those who banked with Bank X were able to handle their finances well enough to be able to afford holidays. These holidays would be seen as strengthing the family unit. This is an extremely important theme for most women and has a very high emotional appeal for every head of a household.

A second ad showed a photo of refreshments at a birthday party with drawings of people standing around the table. This was an emotional appeal to the home-security sense. Even more than the first ad, it had very specific appeal to those customers who had children. The careful juxtaposition of Bank X with a scene of domestic harmony again succeeded in creating the feeling that the bank was a friend. Indeed, one might almost consider inviting the bank staff to a birthday party, so different were they from the standard, stuffy banker stereotypes of the past.

The third picture had the family at a zoo. This again was an effort to include the bank with the family as a helpful friend, a friend who thought that little family outings were important enough to portray in an advertisement which did not even try to sell a service in the same paragraph. A minor point, but one easily missed, was the friendly connection between the zoo at the top of the ad and the many employees at the bottom. Since a zoo implies diversity of animal types, so the photographs indicated a diversity of human types in a warm and sympathetic manner. It was tantamount to saying, "We have everyone from aardvarks to zebras working and banking here, and whatever sort of person you are, you are just as welcome."

The last ad showed a large photograph of a family ready for a camping trip. This one was more directly aimed at the male head of the household, since men often like to rough it in the woods for a holiday, whereas most wives are more attracted to the comforts of home and hotel. It said that Bank X was young at heart and willing to do a bit of pioneering itself. The ad further implied an approval of this sort of recreation for its customers. To have bank backing for a camping trip does a great deal for one's impression of that bank.

It was difficult to make any accurate judgments about which of the advertisements would score the highest on appeal or effectiveness. Such information would be dependent on a large-scale survey and interviews with those who had been exposed to the new advertising. In this case, however, the bank did not desire the sort of study which would have pinpointed exactly which groups of people were responding to which messages.[2]

It seemed to us, however, that each of these advertisements had the attention getting and emotional impact qualities associated with a distinctive campaign to give the bank a favorable public image. Using the same copy theme with a variety of personal situations gave unity to the whole series of advertisements.

Numerous elaborations on these advertising themes could be made. We would have liked to research possible future changes for the main heading "Friends you know work at Bank X." A copy line as direct as that can be endlessly modified for particular emphasis. One such modification could be "Friends you know serve you at X" to underscore the idea of service both to the individual customer and to the community at large. In addition, a more complete study would probably indicate specific situations with high recall that could be included in such advertisements. A more complete study would also have provided helpful information as to how much art work and how much photography should be combined for the greatest possible effect.

We were satisfied with all that had been accomplished by means of a short consultation. Of course, we recommended that the bank embark on a program of copy-testing interviews to further test the results of these new advertisements. A general survey was also suggested to serve not only a measurement of the relative effectiveness of X's advertising as compared with other local banks, but also to serve as a base for future studies when new themes were being tried out. Consulting can get some of the major difficulties ironed out in a general fashion in a short period of time. But we are often more comfortable with the kind of data which results from a careful, detailed, empirical survey.

A considerable body of data from commercial organizations exists showing the extent to which members of the public attend to and remember print advertising. Such research usually shows most consumer product ads scoring higher in readership than ads for banks and insurance companies. The value of studying advertising effectiveness can be put in simple monetary terms. To increase an advertising expenditure in the print media by twenty percent can be quite expensive. To increase the attention-getting power of ads can cost

2. See Grossack, M. (ed) Understanding Consumer Behavior p. 221-229 for a presentation of advertising measurement.

the bank a research or consulting investment from a few hundred up to fifteen hundred dollars for copy testing. But it can lead to a monetary savings for the bank by yielding more return for each dollar spent in advertising. With bank ads frequently being noticed by only five or six percent of the total newspaper readership, a new, psychologically based approach to bank advertising becomes a worthwhile suggestion for progressive bank management.

A study by the Institute for Consumer Psychology concerning four bank retail ads that were copy-tested after their appearance in a newspaper indicates wide differences in the extent to which the ads gained attention, were believed in, and excited reader interest and curiosity. In fact, the differences in ratings among the ads suggest that the proper selection of ads can easily increase the psychological effectiveness of an investment in media by thirty percent or more.

I-C ADVERTISING TEST

The ultimate measurement of advertising effectiveness must be at a psychological level. Mental changes in the recipient of a communication are the results of primary interest to the advertiser.

The *I-C Advertising Test* (image credibility) rests on the premise that ad effectiveness must be measured scientifically as well as meaningfully. This test provides quantative measurement of five variables using projective attitude scales, which makes it possible to develop comparable norms for companies, various ads, and types of respondents. The variables (selected on the basis of interviews and advertising executives) are: *image:* to what extent does the ad develop a favorable perception of the company and product, *credibility:* is the ad believed, *attention-getting:* how noticeable and striking is it, *emotional impact:* does the ad reduce respondent resistance and produce a pleasant feeling in the respondent, and *action-potential:* does the ad produce a responsiveness and readiness to act.

The actual procedure is first to determine by open-end interview briefly product preferences in the area of investigation and ad recall. Then the interviewee is allowed to view the ad without a time limit (except for TV film) and his reactions (feelings and comprehension) are elicited. Then the *I-C Test* is given. Post-test interview probes test responses. Validity has been established by satisfactory comparison of pre- and post-interview data with test responses to each variable.

The value in pre-testing television or printed advertisements can be seen in a study (Table 1) of four printed bank advertisements shown to 80 respondents in a random sample of dwelling units. Scores represent the number of people affected by each variable in a positive direction. By eliminating Ad A from his campaign, the client was able to save money and realize a greater psychological return.

It is believed that this test can effect savings for all advertisers. The administration can be by trained field interviewers. Qualitative comments suggest hypotheses for changes in future advertising copy, making the test useful for pre-tests of ads in layout form and of television storyboards and films. It pinpoints strengths and weaknesses of ads and allows for meaningful comparison with competitive ads.

TABLE 1
Frequency of Favorable Responses to Four Bank Advertisements (N = 80)

Variables	Ad A	Ad B	Ad C	Ad D
Image	42	52	62	60
Action-potential	26	42	42	44
Impact	44	58	66	66
Credibility	40	60	64	66
Attention-getting	30	44	50	52

From *Psychological Reports,* 1960, 7, 486. ©Southern Universities Press 1960.

VII
RESEARCHING THE PSYCHOLOGY
OF RETAIL BANKING*

I. BASIC APPROACH TO THIS STUDY

As in all practical studies, the purpose of this proposed research is to find clear-cut, concrete answers to business problems. Toward that end we combine psychological knowledge and tools of the behavioral sciences with experience in business. Our procedures are basically psychological, and our goals include developing the situational context and hypotheses from which creative new ideas and approaches may be derived. In this era of increasingly sharp competition, every American business needs new tools for achieving prominence in the market and for helping management to chart its course of action with greater accuracy. Proper findings must be presented in clear and simple language, and they should act as a stimulus to independent policy-making and creativity in advertising and selling.

II. OBJECTIVES

Underlying Psychology in Commercial Banking:
Some Opinions and Questions

Taking the point of view of the retail customer, we will ascertain the extent to which a bank relationship is important and, more basically, whether it is something that exists in fantasy or in actual practice. For example, does it matter really where one gets his gasoline? It may if the customer feels he is important to the vendor — if he feels that he is accepted with courtesy and warmth, especially in emergencies.

Is it Utopian for a bank to try to foster those resources which offer some type of personal banking relationship? Obviously, the advertising should create the *fantasy* of stability, dependency, security and *help when needed.*

*This is an example of how a research program was actually formulated and presented to a prospective client.

This is important to most people, since their main banking activities are checking, savings, and loans. Relatively few will ask a banker for advice on insurance policies, tax returns, or travel plans, unless these services are established more concretely in their minds. The most important point for effective advertising is, however, that the customer need not feel anxious about the bank's acceptance of him. Our research will pinpoint certain key questions along this line clearly, concisely and without equivocation:

Do people want a bank to offer them something more than simple services obtainable anywhere: checking accounts, loans, and savings accounts?

What are the other things people need, wish they had and want?

Which of these should the bank offer in advertising, and how should these needs be fulfilled in practice?

To what extent should a commercial bank be a multi-service center for financial help and to what extent would people be willing to pay for this kind of relationship?

Which kinds of people would be most likely to pay for these services?

Useful research should also spell out the unfulfilled needs of different classes of customers and define kinds of actions that would most appeal to each segment of the population — to each age group, family condition, occupational level, and life style. In this anxious world a bank fulfills certain needs for people: a bank means stability, reassurance and confidence; it is something that keeps running smoothly through good times and bad, war and peace. How can a commercial bank make the man on the street share this feeling of stability? Should it do so? The research under consideration must have a stronger psychological orientation than research conducted on the business community. Business men have more intense banking needs. Their operations are intimately associated with their commercial banking relationships. Therefore, it is possible to utilize a more structured, factual approach in studying the business community.

Let us, for example, think of a progressive bank in 1980. Who will be the prime customers for its retail business then? Who will be most susceptible to picking a new bank, most open-minded? This research must give careful consideration to the so-called youth market, those not yet committed to a particular banking connection. Do these younger people pick their bank on the basis of recommendations of parents, friends, associates or the influence of advertising? To what extent are they likely to seek out the bank nearest their home or place of employment? An analytical appraisal of this problem indicates that certain other questions are in order also:

1. Does the bank cater to a clientele different from that of its competitors? Are the bank's subject customers more sophisticated? Younger? More conscious of what a bank may do for them? More attracted to the modern image of a television campaign?

2. Are educational loans something that should be a focal point in advertising and marketing strategy? A proper psychological study must consider also the emotional and social problems that impinge on business activity. We know that college costs are rising, that education after high school is something the vast majority aspires to, and that soon junior college enrollment will surpass that of four year schools. Should there be a tie in with this social trend and thus with the retail market of today and tomorrow?

3. What are the appeals most likely to effect change in banking connection? How can the decision-making process in retail bank selection be best influenced by a customer-oriented bank. How can a more personal bank help to maintain customer loyalty?

Retail Image of Commercial Banks

We have, at this time, substantial documentation of the images held by business people of the major Boston banks. On that basis, we can assume that, in general, the image suitable for business accounts is not one suitable for retail. The retail customer is usually part of a family, not a business. He is usually employed by others, not himself, and concerned with loans of under $3,500 — not the sizable amounts required for commercial investment. The psychology involved in gaining his loyalty must be different. We must learn how he sees each of the major banks. Can he name them and what comes to mind about each? What type of personality does he associate with each? For the retail customer the teller is of crucial importance for he is his major banking contact. How are the tellers rated at each bank and what more might one expect from them? We also want this study to indicate what the customer may find unsatisfactory about the teller and the banking situation. One example is a customer complaining that he had to go to three different windows to get a form filled out correctly; another that he wanted to transact business on a loan form but found the teller unable to handle it.

The retail image will be investigated in terms of the ideal image a bank should have. This will differ for certain segments of the population, but the research will indicate the common points and differences in ideal image for different segments of the market. It will recommend the personality a bank should develop for its retail market, as well as indicate competitive strengths and weaknesses of all leading banks in a given market area.

Savings and Loan Accounts

How does the commercial bank fit in with the other available sources for savings accounts and loans? This is a crucial question. Thus we must learn the extent to which savings banks are used for borrowing by attempting to answer the following questions:

1. What is the image of the savings bank versus the commercial bank as a place for savings accounts?
2. How do people regard the loan company, savings bank, and commercial bank as sources for borrowing money?
3. How effective has the advertising been for the leading savings banks?
4. How effective has the advertising been for the finance companies?
5. How much reluctance is there among different categories of people in approaching the commercial bank for money? How much fear and suspicion is there of the loan company?
6. How much concern and awareness is there of differences in interest rates paid by savings banks and commercial banks?
7. How widely known is it that commercial banks offer savings accounts, and why haven't more loan customers had savings accounts with the bank?
8. What are the attractions and strengths, liabilities and weaknesses of the various competitors in the savings account field? In the personal loan field?

Checking Accounts

1. How aware are residents of "free" checking services?
2. How can customers of competitors be attracted to free checking?
3. What might be done to enhance the appeal of free checking? To further differentiate it from the competition?

Cross-Selling

We want to find out from the people we interview the extent to which they have been approached for savings accounts and loans by banks with whom they have checking accounts. We want to know whether the cross-selling of the competition has been active or passive? We need to know how savings accounts are distributed in the population, the extent to which customers of each bank also have savings accounts in commercial banks as well as in savings and cooperative banks. How do they decide whether to save where they check and borrow? What considerations are important? Is "full service" an important concept, and what does this term mean to people — especially since you can usually find a savings bank, commercial bank, and loan company suite located near one another.

It is important for a bank to design special service packages to facilitate cross-selling? What should these be like? What needs do different types of consumers have that can be appealed to by cross-selling? What percent of the population has safe-deposit boxes, needs them, or can be persuaded of their utility?

Retail Bank Advertising

In general, our findings on other studies indicate that non-business people listen less to local bank advertising and remember it less perfectly than do their counterparts in business. In fact, most people are somewhat disinterested in bank advertising. Our studies in the retail banking field indicate at least that the majority of people will have no specific recall of advertising for commercial banks. What recall there is shows poor differentiation between one bank and the next. We have done some work in considering the kinds of retail bank ads that would be most memorable, since it is the intent of the research to generate specific image-building recommendations. In fact, there usually is more than one possible advertising approach that might be worth considering. For example, there is possibly a drawback in having a business-oriented bank name. Does a word connoting business cause some people to hesitate about approaching the bank? This is a matter of such importance that it might be worth some very serious consideration as part of the research endeavor.

It is important to humanize further in the eyes of the retail public in a way that is credible, without leading to unreal expectations from the public. The desired image should mainly reinforce the idea that customers are important to banks and that all are welcome. Our study will yield, not only possible advertising lines in order of their importance, but specific ideas on how those lines might be meaningfully elaborated to the public, to obtaining involvement and a favorable reaction.

Bank Credit Cards

This study will also seek information about utilizing credit cards rather than obtaining loans directly. The impact of bank credit cards on the retail image of its issuing bank will be a secondary area of investigation, and the concept of each local bank as a loan source will be evaluated carefully to learn whether various segments of the population feel that certain banks are more ready to "grant" loans to consumers than others. For example, our feeling is that some banks may be viewed as less accessible to borrowing than are their competitor banks. If this is so, the research will suggest ways of dealing with this issue.

Competitive Appeals

Just as we will obtain a valid reading of the effectiveness and implications of the competitions' campaign, we will also obtain a measurement of the recall, credibility, and effectiveness of the "slogans." The use of slogans was one of the earliest attempts to dislodge the commercial bank from its rigid, authoritarian mold. The extent to which this has helped banks' images will be determined. Within this context our studies suggest a suspicious consumer attitude concerning the friendliness of banks. A feeling seems prevalent that banks are fair weather friends, not friends when in actual need — especially as far as loans go.*

An experimental slogan — "we know what you want from a bank" — will be evaluated impartially and in depth. Preliminary evaluation of this term seems to indicate that it is too abstract and general; perhaps it's meaningless and connotes nothing of value to the consumer. Our preliminary hypothesis is that it is not a suitable slogan. We hope that other concepts will be offered for evaluation as research starts and that new ones will emerge before the study ends from the results obtained in the interviews.

Word of Mouth in Retail Banking

It will be an important matter to determine the extent to which retail banking is influenced by word of mouth communications about where to open checking and savings accounts and where to obtain loans. The research will study the entire decision making process relevant to the specific bank. It will pinpoint action strategies to maximize the effective communication of appeals in advertising and the internal operation of bank branches to facilitate account acquisition and maintenance.

Spokesmen in Bank Advertising

Our firm has developed ways to pre-test the effectiveness of potential spokesmen on advertising impact. This has been done by presenting planned series of advertisements to samples of people in an experimental fashion. It is possible for a bank to answer key questions about potential spokesmen, concerning their credibility and influence potential for different market segments. Some spokesmen have impact for businessmen, but not for retail customers and vice-versa. The strategy implications of this dilemma will be worked out in comprehensive fashion.

Account Turnover

Research presently available indicates that the typical commercial bank loses anywhere from 18% to 22% of savings and checking accounts annually. At the same time, new accounts are secured which usually make up for the losses. It would seem to us that a bank can benefit from learning about some of the factors that help deter account turnover. Our study will take this problem into consideration. Much account loss appears to be unnecessary and

---

*The pilot studies done as part of this study suggest that retail customers are somewhat less hostile towards banks than, say, ten years ago.

not the result of mere "convenience." There is also some evidence that account turnover varies in a definable way. This evidence would suggest that certain market techniques should be planned to capitalize on seasonal tendencies, since changes in accounts are more likely to occur in some months than in others.

Summary of Problem Areas

The kinds of problems about which we expect to have reliable information include:

1. Present image of each major commercial bank held by each important population group
2. Factors associated with the image of each bank
3. Awareness of each bank
4. Experiences at each bank
5. Decision-making process in selection of bank
6. Unfulfilled needs in banking, and areas for new bank activity
7. Appeals of commercial banks to retail publics
8. Unfavorable feelings about each commercial bank
9 Experience and usage of checking account, account turnover
10. "Convenience" as a problem, with ways to combat weakness of client in number of branches
11. Appeals of after-hour banking, bank by mail, automobile tellers
12. Awareness of savings account service at commercial bank and reasons for not using savings accounts at commercial banks, ways to develop savings account business
13. Action recommendation for bank advertising and marketing in areas of image-making, advertising appeals, advertising style and approach, new services, in-bank promotional activities, approaches to checking, loans, and savings fields, as well as deposit boxes
14. Approach to the whole concept of the bank as a "system" offering financial services; ways to help develop a "package" for meeting needs and how to implement the "package" services
15. Specific unfilled needs for financial counsel
16, Favorable and unfavorable feelings associated with each bank
17. "Full-Service" concept
18. Awareness of services offered at commercial banks and their cost
19. Emotional relationship of consumer to banks (present and desired)
20. Attitudes towards savings banks
21. Comparisons of savings banks with commercial banks
22. Attitudes towards the usage of finance companies
23. Factors encouraging and hindering usage of bank by mail

III. COMMENTS AND SAMPLING

In planning a research program for a bank we would expect probability study to yield less useful material than a selective sample. Further, we believe in weighing the number of interviews in terms of the importance of specific types of people to the bank's goals and needs.

Who Should be Studied?

It seems most feasible to stress the interviews with people who live or work in the bank's own city. Suburban interviews would only be of value, if the interviewees worked locally or already had dealings with another bank in the same community. Therefore, it would seem that the sample should be selected with exact care. Were this not done, twenty-five percent of the investment would be worthless because people could be interviewed whose feelings are insignificant in the present action strategies of the bank. Other people should automatically be sampled less frequently in the survey, e.g., those without any present checking or savings account, those over 55, who are less likely to switch than those younger and should be under-represented in the final selection of respondents. It is often only minimally helpful to study many people on a simple statistical basis, and we recommend that banks would often gain fuller benefits by studying fewer people with more intensity.

An adequate psychological approach would work in stages:

1. The search for hypotheses from the point of view of the people being studied
2. The exploration of issues and areas deemed most significant by the bank as well as our findings
3. The gradual development of an instrument that uses interview data to solve problems and discover new ones
4. Interviews *should be conducted in waves* rather than in one batch
5. Three waves of intensive interviews should be considered:

   a. *wave one:* exploratory phase (seventy interviews)
      35 male – 35 female
      35 upper and middle income – 35 working class lower-middle
      45 center of community area – 25 distributed approaching limits of community
      15 age 21 to 34; 25 age 35 to 50; and 15 over age 50

   All respondents presently would have a checking account. Each interview would be psychologically oriented, lasting approximately two hours.

b. *wave two:* validation phase (seventy interviews)
The analysis of (wave one) material yields conclusions on topics and areas requiring additional study. From this material seventy more hour-long psychological interviews are conducted to test certain hypotheses.

c. *wave three:* action phase
Up to four hundred additional interviews are conducted to test out conclusively all questions still unanswered and to yield definite strategy recommendations. The sampling must be adequate to test out the bank's objectives and reliably assess the relevant publics of the bank. These interviews should be about one hour in length. Interviews are conducted evenings and weekends to insure obtaining an adequate sample of men. Interviewers do their work in pre-selected geographical areas, lessening freedom of choice in respondent selection. The kinds of people we study and about whom we thus have reliable information will include:

- men
- women
- persons central to the bank's location
- peripheral individuals
- customers of each major competing bank.
- customers of banks in surburban communities.
- youth market
- younger families
- middle-aged families
- older families
- middle class and affluent people
- lower middle class and working people
- ethnic groups
- loan customers of commercial banks and other loan sources
- checking customers
- savings customers of commercial banks and other banks
- those aware of bank advertising
- sophisticated consumers, opinion leaders, ambitious, mobile people
- conventional people who are less amenable to change

The Question of Social Class

This proposed research will take into account the question of social class differences in the orientation of urban and suburban residents. More specifically, the fact that cities can be predominantly working class and lower-middle class while suburbs are more affluent need not preclude the development of an appeal that cuts across social lines. One is the appeal of "getting ahead." Just as the banker has used his image as the friend of business progress so might he consider expanding this idea to include the individual retail customer. If the bank is interested, we will test out the implications of this appeal. Getting ahead is associated with savings, with having extra money for the nicer things in life, with easily obtaining loans when needed. This idea of personal social mobility is deeply rooted in the social fabric of our culture and ties in with the trend to extend economic advantages to more segments of the population.

Obviously, there are important social class differences in attitudes towards savings, money, the use of discretionary income, attitudes towards borrowing, etc. This literature is well known to our firm and should be utilized in the study.

We cannot ignore the fact of ethnic groups in the city. The extent to which this deters or helps a particular bank is a matter of possible interest to the study. The psychological approach will yield information as to the way each bank is seen in relation to the ethnic balance of its employees, the appeal of the bank to ethnic groups, and the forces at work that should be recognized as relevant to considerations for action.

IV. METHODS FOR CONDUCTING THE STUDY

Individuals conducting psychological interviews should have some experience and should also be given special training for this study. Since the questions we have posed, and the research areas we propose to explore concern basic human motivations, we will employ techniques developed in the fields of psychology and related sciences.* These techniques have been developed and tested by our organization over a twelve-year period in commercial research problems.

Depth Interviews

Unlike conventional research, which asks direct questions, in depth interviewing specialists should encourage respondents to express freely all their feelings and associations about a given subject, to ramble on about all their experiences in dealing with the subject. This provides an insight into the real motivations and the underlying factors involved.

Projective Tests

During the course of the investigation projective questionnaires and visual stimuli should be developed. These would contain an unstructured type of

*These techniques are described in "Understanding Consumer Behavior," pages 183 - 230. Christopher Publishers, No. Quincy, Mass; 1966.

question, in response to which the respondent projects his real emotions and feelings about commercial banking.

Group Interviews

Group interviews are becoming increasingly important in consumer psychological studies. These insure that our clients readily learn how people feel (from their own voices) without biasing the questions, without assumptions as to what is important or unimportant to them. Group interviews help to guage the attitudes that are most important to investigate among larger numbers of people. These interviews can be of significant value in developing the specific program most suitable to your needs. They often reveal the basic attitudes in the population and give new leads for areas of study that are not anticipated beforehand. Moreover, such groups help to pilot-test techniques and strategies of interviewing. Hearing them helps the client involve himself in the study and contribute more thinking to the ultimate study and its objectives.

Client Involvement

Client participation in all phases of the study should be encouraged. We know from experience that adequate research cannot be conducted in an ivory tower. Every client has limitations of policy, and many considerations preclude certain actions in marketing and advertising. Certain subtleties must be taken into account. These intimate communications between client and researcher help make for a more useful final product.

Continual Cross-Validation

By conducting the research in waves of interviews and by using a variety of questions, techniques, and approaches on the same problems, we obtain a validity that is not available in a utilization of one instrument on one sample in one time phase. A multi-dimensional study systematically approaches the problems from the general to the specific in a gradual approximation of scientific truths concerning the city's retail banking. It is unique in design, scope, and methodology. The approaches are geared to psychological theory and the orientation is towards actionable business strategy.

Psychological Versus Statistical Research in Retail Banking

It would be very easy to propose the development of a survey instrument and a questionnaire for use on a representative sample of five hundred people that can be computerized readily. The research of this type can, of course, include open-ended questions, but such a study at this point would be psychologically inadequate and would be unable to relate the needs and problems of the public to potential avenues of bank action. So the research on a more psychological basis is proposed as a more meaningful avenue. The sample will be more meaningful as it is pinpointed towards the potential market of the bank, which, by many criteria, obviously differs from the population at large.

The final study proposed would include information based on *at least* 540 interviews, more intensive and valuable than can be obtained in any traditional approach. If deemed advisable, more interviews can be conducted on specific target groups. Final sampling decisions should be judiciously based on pre-test findings as well as results of the first wave of interviews.

Computer Analysis

Interview data can be computerized, if deemed necessary, with the assistance of a computer service company which has considerable experience in handling marketing and psychological data as well as patented program systems that may be applicable to the bank's data. The computer analysis will permit breakdowns of the interviews by sex, age, income level, attitude and awareness questions, bank used, and whatever other pertinent categories emerge in the course of preliminary trial analyses of the data. Psychological information concerning the respondents will be built into the final instrument and utilized in computer analysis.

V. FINAL REPORT

Our findings and the supporting evidence will be submitted to you together with a:

Blue Print for Action

The blue print for action will describe the practical application of our research findings to the problems of the bank. Any report, to be of full value, must spell out ways and means of utilizing the findings to the greatest possible advantage.

Personal Consultation

This will be for the purpose of discussing all aspects of the report and clarification of any questions relating to the findings, their practical application or their creative translations into actual advertising, sales and promotional programs.

VI. TIME

It is difficult to set *exact* delivery dates for reports, due to the fact that sometimes tentative findings develop in the course of conducting the study and require unexpected time consuming validation. We estimate, however, that the time required to complete a study such has been discussed herein would be, approximately four months.

VII. EXPLORATORY PILOT STUDIES

As part of this presentation, the Institute has conducted a group-depth interview and twenty-two pilot individual interviews. The data from these ventures has yet to be analyzed completely, but certain hypotheses are emerging concerning retail banking. Obviously, these preliminary impressions have to be validated on a large scale basis:

Hypotheses from One Group Interview

1. There are more complaints about Bank Y than any of the other banks. These include errors of a clerical nature, refusal of reasonable loan requests, refusal to cash checks of customers at a different branch of the bank, etc.
2. By far, the banks with the most branches have the greatest number of accounts and are seen as most convenient. There is a strong appeal for drive-in banking, after-hour banking and Saturday banking.
3. Bank X advertising is rated favorably and remembered well, but in the eyes of the consumer the bank has a business image and is not seen as actively pursuing the interests of the average person.
4. There are some suspicions and resistances to free checking, perpetuated by the feeling that the bank is still making money on the customer and that it is better to keep your checking account lower than $100. This feeling, however, may only be prevalent in certain segments of the population.
5. Bank Z's retail image has been augmented by BankAmericard, which is highly approved by its users. Its image on the retail market is youth-oriented in that BankAmericard has a strong appeal for younger borrowers.
6. The major banks are not seen as aloof and stuffy, but as friendly and caring. Although consumers feel that big business is more important to the bank than they are, they also feel that they are getting attention from the banks. The typical respondent is now less hostile to banks than we found in our first banking studies in 1958 and 1959.
7. Those interviewed are not certain whether checking accounts are insured.
8. Although interest rate plays a strong part in savings accounts, proximity is as important as well as a long personal history (in many cases from childhood) of dealing with particular savings bank.
9. There is very little cross-selling of bank services to the retail public.

10. Right now, Bank X has the weakest consumer franchise by far of the four leading banks in Boston.

11. It is quite likely that an effective appeal to the retail market by Bank X will involve significant changes in overall advertising strategy in order to be successful. It would be unreal to expect more than a gradual increase in market share of retail customers.

12. Numerous suggestions are offered in the group interviews:
    a. special deposit windows for business accounts requiring much time
    b. free checking in exchange for having a savings account at the bank
    c. balance overdrafts with money from savings accounts
    d. automatically take savings and loan payments out of checking account

13. The concept of a personal banker suits the public taste; however, the average respondent does not expect *complete* financial advice. He expects investment advice from his customer's man, real estate advice from a savings bank. The idea of having an accessible bank official (stressed in Y's advertising) has appeal and merit, and it is noteworthy that Bank Y did not lose the customers we interviewed who complained about the bank. The areas of personal counsel would have to be explored in depth.

14. Banks are not seen as having enough genuine interest in personal loans. Those interviewed do not see savings banks for personal loans except on passbooks and home improvements. The feeling was expressed in our group that Bank W and Bank Z are more interested in lending money than the other two banks.

15. Those interviewed assume they need not be a bank customer to borrow money from a bank, and this expectation can lead to disenchantment, e.g., one bank Z customer who was refused loan by Bank Y for a small amount because he didn't change his checking account and savings to Y from Z. He went to Y because he had heard their rate of interest was lower.

16. The bank that really makes the consumer feel loans are easy will have an important selling point. The first bank loan experience is a threat and test of maturity and acceptance. We have comments on the difficulties of getting credit and loans when first married, and this area of appeal is worth considering. The loan area requires psychological approaches that are quite subtle.

17. It is common to have more than one checking account and deal with a bank near home and one near work. The savings account is likely to be near home. Bank by mail may be more accepted now for savings than checking accounts.

18. There tends to be little shopping around for the best interest on loans.
19. The feeling was expressed in the group that commercial banks can play a useful role in helping take the disadvantaged out of the clutches of finance companies, especially if the borrower has a decent credit record and is employed. There is a fear of loan refusal still prevalent among large segments of the retail public.
20. It would appear offbeat, but the banking habits of women may be an important leverage for bank X, since none of the banks are appealing to the growing economic emancipation of women with their discretionary incomes. This is a field that should be studied very carefully. Our preliminary findings certainly suggest an important role for the wife in handling the savings accounts and in many cases her own checking account, especially if she works at least part-time.
21. The group interview suggests that more and more people, despite their resistances, will be drawn to free checking accounts. There is a strong awareness of numerous banks offering this service.

Hypotheses from Individual Depth Interviews

The individual depth interviews were conducted with twenty-two people. These interviews were exploratory in nature. They serve to validate some of the suggestions emerging from the first group interview and offer other insights:

1. Again we have more complaints about X than any other bank. These complaints include the arrogance of the employees, rudeness of a branch manager, and long lines at windows. The individual interviews suggest that there has been some switching from Y to W that may be a pattern among certain segments of the market or near certain branches. The individual interviews show that Z has a credit card system that has augmented its image. It also is seen as a family bank and as one for younger people. The majority of those interviewed individually who had opinions about X see it as a business bank, where loans are easy for business. We must state that large numbers of retail customers are not knowledgeable or interested in banks, and their recall is far weaker than that of businessmen.
2. Those interviewed in this phase were influenced mostly by the location of the branch in making their choice. Word of mouth was of little importance. Once a customer, they appear most concerned with a friendly attitude on the part of tellers and getting their business done quickly. Some become checking customers of a bank after getting their car loan at the suggestion of a dealer. Just as do businessmen, retail customers feel loyal to their bank and secure when they feel known in

the local branch. Also, there is a feeling that changing one's bank is cumbersome. The individual interviews focused on second choices and the pattern of choices tended to leave X fourth, with most customers considering only the other three banks. The need for more personal attention seemed the kind of reason, not yet validated, that would most make a person want to leave (assuming the move is not related to new housing, job location, or loan refusal).

3. The majority appear to be aware of free checking, and those who know of it are more aware of X than of any other bank. However, most respondents can also name at least two banks offering the service if they are aware of the service at all. There are many interesting motivations around free checking service:

    a. Some individuals are frugal and cost conscious.

    b. Others are simply consumption conscious, changing banks for free checking would not be worth the bother to them.

    c. Another pattern of feelings is expressed by those who already have friends at a given bank or are already loan customers there.

    d. Surprisingly, hostility to banks comes out most readily on discussions of this area (the way our pilot tests were set up). The feeling is expressed that people are entitled to free checking just because they are already bank customers and that banks make enough on them anyway. Consequently, there is some resistance to the $100 minimum.

4. About half the people we talked with do not like to bank by mail, but approximately half do find it convenient and pleasant. We would guess that at least twenty percent of the retail banking public is susceptible to banking by mail. However, large numbers want to execute their business on the spot. The are unconfortable waiting to get their deposit slip back in the mail, and some distrust the mail.

5. Consumers often have a hard time differentiating one bank's advertising from another's. For example, our interviews find five people associating Y's slogan with Bank W. This service (one of personal advice) appears to have the following patterns of reactions:

    a. About a third are really attracted to having someone at the bank whom they know and whom they feel knows them. The opportunity for personal consultation and advice and financial help is something a significant element in the population wants.

    b. Other respondents feel that this is just an advertising game.

    c. Many Y customers feel that the bank is not equipped to give this advice, and certain officers are disliked by customers there.

    d. Other respondents feel the service is mainly geared to businessmen, not the average family.

This is a basic area of investigation, because our pilot tests show that large numbers of people want to feel they know someone at the bank personally in order to increase their feelings of esteem and security, to help in any business decisions that confront them, to help establish credit and advice on expenditures, to give help when travelling abroad, and to feel they are getting the prestige of attention from a banker.

6. Our evidence suggests that word of mouth does play a part in selection of the bank for *obtaining a loan.* We find borrowing on a savings passbook one of the favorite methods employed and another important pattern is associated with the bank which finances a car loan. People appear to feel that they want credit established and are reluctant to seek out commercial banks for their very first loan. There is a feeling that appears in our interviews that commercial banks charge more for loans than do savings banks and are less accessible to the average person. Credit Unions emerge in our preliminary work as an inportant area of securing loans for several of the respondents. People are interested in how much the loan will cost. Commercial banks, especially W, are seen as convenient for making payments on loans.

7. The convenience of checking and saving at the same place is mentioned as a major reason for having savings accounts at commercial banks. Most reasons given for saving elsewhere are higher interest rates, long personal history with the savings bank, and the feeling that the savings bank is more pleasant.

8. Further exploration of the concept of convenience indicates that this connotes: closeness to home, closeness to work, helpful tellers, Saturday hours, drive-in banking, plenty of parking, special lines for quick deposits, longer banking hours, chairs for waiting, etc.

9. Our results indicate from this pretest that the major complaints with retail banking currently centers around the teller's window — complain long waiting or unfriendly reception. This merits study.

10. There is still some desire among a certain segment for the "checkless society" with the commercial bank automatically paying one's utilities, rent, insurance, and other bills.

11. Our research utilized a sematic differential image test (a special kind of attitude scale similar to that in our business study) on retail customers. Suffice it to say no that the majority of interviewees were customers of Banks W and X and that:

    1. There is high awareness and favorable reaction to Bank X's television work.
    2. People still see Bank X as appealing more to business more than does the competition.

3. Bank X, is associated with wealth on our pretests.
4. Despite the complaints aboutBank Y, it still has a strong image. Bank X has the weakest retail image of the four banks tested.
5. Bank Z and W have by far the best ratings on our retail image questions.

VIII. INTEGRATION OF PRETEST FINDINGS

Should a bank commission a special study for its own needs, the Institute will carefully study the results already available. This will afford a considerable savings of time and money and enable the research to begin with a clearer perspective of all issues involved. However, the information available is essentially pretest findings which are illustrative. They do not include all problem areas which could be specified by any and every bank. Nor did the pretest sample all segments of the population considered important or utilize all our techniques of psychological testing.

VIII

THE CITIZEN'S NATIONAL BANK:
A STUDY IN COMMERCIAL BANKING*

Most people involved in a certain business have gained, by their association with it, a sensitivity for the sort of actions which will aid in its growth and development. It doesn't take a consumer survey to help a soft drink bottler to decide to put on an extra shift during the summer months. Everybody who gets hot likes to cool off, and opinion in that area is unanimous enough to be considered obvious. After a few years in the business, moreover, the owner of such an operation would begin to see relationships between vacation time, temperature heights, and the consumption of soft drinks. But this is a very simple form of predicting the customer's wants and needs.

In many other areas, however, an empirical study can significantly aid the decision-making process. What this means, simply, is that when you get into areas which are more abstract than simple physical wants, the factors controlling consumption are not as easy to recognize or predict. The average business does not, for example, open its doors only in a given month, nor is there any sure means of predicting the rate at which it will grow. Beyond that, there is a host of subjective factors by which the operator of the business judges what help he will need and when. It is easy to predict that most people will get thirsty in the summer, but there is no sure way to determine in advance either when or how a business or an individual will require the services of a bank.

The most obvious way for a banker to deal with this lack of information would be to advertise all his services, everywhere, all the time. But this would be both prohibitively expensive and time-consuming. We have to determine, then, into which general and specific areas we can concentrate our sales effort without each day actually asking each account holder, or prospective account holder, what their pleasure would be. Here we run into a little difficulty.

*Assumed names are used throughout this essay.

Individuals involved in enterprise develop their own attitudes as to how to run the show. After a time, one eventually gets a feel for his business climate and can, to a large extent, predict what course of action to take without relying on a lot of advice from those not as close to his situation. When this means trying to make a decision on how to predict another's psychological wants or needs, it becomes a matter of extreme subtlety. It is easy to say that all businessmen need a good banking connection, but it is not so easy for one man, or for a group of men to estimate just how this service should be offered. What might seem a friendly stance to one customer would appear ingratiating to another. A conservative stance can appear dependable to some observers and cold to others. Here is where some consensus of opinion is needed.

A bank officer might realize that entry into the bank credit card market is not only profitable for his bank, but inevitable if his bank is to keep up with our growing economy. However, he also remembers that the mythical Mr. Dowell of the Universal Manufacturing Company always pays cash for his purchases, and he has always considered credit cards as a temptation to the financially insecure to get into debt with the issuing company, thus insuring continual patronage. But the bank officer's clear head tells him that bank credit cards are a logical, profitable, and altogether sound area for the growth of banking services. Mr. Dowell's equally clear head (he can size up the statewide demand for medium widgets with three phone calls and a roll of the dice) tells him that anyone, including bank officers, who indulge in promoting credit cards are about a half step from being loan sharks.

The problem is, how many Mr. Dowells are there in your banking area? With whom do they bank, and can they be educated? Or are they so fixed in their ideas that the mere mention of credit cards would invite a blast of invective? How many accounts would your bank stand to lose if you added this service, and how would this stack up against the expected return? Here is where a carefully structured consumer attitude survey can provide extremely helpful data. The countless interviews, taken one by one, are not of great help, but skilled interpretation of the data is a valuable tool for getting a better feel for your whole area. Bearing in mind that the average bank officer knows what is best for his bank, it would be nice to know what his customers think would be best for the bank. Even though the average customer has nowhere near the education or experience to delve into these matters, he probably has some firm thoughts about them. And it is not uncommon for a man to take his business elsewhere if, for some reason, he thinks that his bank is not doing its job well, or perhaps that another bank is doing it better.

This, then, should be the role of the survey. Most banks are fairly in step with the times and economic conditions. But before advertising or promoting new ideas or services, there should be some reassurance that the customer knows what is actually being done. This information can only be obtained by thoroughly questioning an adequate sample of individuals who are carefully selected to comprise a customer and non-customer cross-section. The answers may often indicate that the plans already agreed upon are indeed correct, but, then again, most people with fire insurance never have a fire. *It's far better to know that you've assessed the situation correctly than to be fairly sure that you know your market and go ahead with an expensive sales campaign, only to discover that you were almost correct.* Simple facts can be easily ignored in the flash of inspiration. For example, because one large midwestern bank quite accurately judged that bank age indicated reliability in the minds of most of its customers, it celebrated its century mark with an extensive multi-media campaign in order to emphasize its one hundred years of service; its top competitor, meanwhile, made the same point by doing nothing but plastering every billboard around with the one sentence message "108 years old."

In the early sixties, we conducted a study for a sizeable metropolitan bank, which we shall call the Citizens National Bank. Our goal was to help them determine how area businessmen were reacting to their recent efforts to step up their service, complete with a new line of television advertisements. With information gained from the preliminary interviews we were able to structure a study which we felt would yield some important information as to how the bank was being seen in relation to the other large banks in the area, and, more specifically, how the public and specific market segmets were responding to the new advertising.

At the time of the study, the greatest competition came from three other metropolitan banks, all of which were larger than Citizen's National. The Security Trust Company was the largest and oldest bank in the area. Because of its size and its reputation, it had a great many commercial accounts. It was generally seen as solid and dependable as well as prestigious, almost a banker's bank. The next largest was the Colony Commercial Bank, which had almost as many branches as Security. Colony had been an active advertiser for years, although its messages seemed to be aimed more at the retail customer. The imposing head of Governor Brewster of the Mayflower colony was a familiar sight on billboards and in other advertising media. There was also the First Trust Company, a bank with a reputation of conservatism and stability. It was somewhat smaller than either Security or Colony and roughly the same size as Citizen's National.

It was hoped that the study would uncover the prevailing attitudes towards these banks and their advertising, and at the same time learn how far Citizen's had come in its efforts to develop a distinct and modern image. It was thought that the information gained would be especially helpful for those planning future marketing and advertising strategies and would, moreover, serve as a base for comparison with future studies. A structured, projective questionnaire was developed and pretested on fifty businessmen. During the second stage of the survey, more than five hundred interviews were collected in such a way as to insure that every business in the metropolitan area would have an equal chance of being called on. The sample was drawn from industries listed in the state directory of industries, Poor's directory, and other sources. Each interviewer was assigned a geographic area and specific companies to interview. In addition, interviewers were given an incentive to call on larger, more inaccessible companies. They were further instructed to interview only the individual in the company most responsible for the financial decisions of the firm. In over half the cases, this meant arranging appointments in advance or making calls twice if the man they wished to see was otherwise occupied.

The disguised figures which we will use are based on the results of these interviews. After computer breakdown and analysis, we were able to prepare almost eighty pages of tables which provided some surprising results. Since many firms used more than one bank, the numbers will occasionally add to more than the total number of interviews. To aid in obtaining a clear picture of attitudes, we considered a firm as the customer of a bank if it dealt only with that bank exclusively. By eliminating multiple bank users from some questions, we were able to obtain a more definitive picture. In evaluating results, one should keep in mind that most people, including businessmen, tend to have more favorable opinions towards those firms with which they have chosen to do business. Most bank customers are, therefore, more aware of their own bank's advertising than of the advertising of others.

When we questioned these businessmen we tried to learn how they felt towards various banks — not by asking them to come up with descriptive phrases, but by offering them a list of forty seven general traits and allowing them to assign these traits to the banks which they felt most exemplified them. One result of this technique was that one could attribute a large number of traits to any one bank if he so desired.

The results showed fairly conclusively that certain of these traits were commonly associated with certain banks. This indicated that the average businessman does indeed have a preconceived notion of the "personality" of the banks with which he is somewhat familiar. It would be easy for any outsider to read through the following list and deduce the general reputation of the banks which were covered in the study:

1. **Security Trust Company** (disguised data)
   - largest
   - for older companies
   - foreign department
   - deals mostly with big companies
   - exclusive
2. **Colony Commercial Bank**
   - friendly
   - most advertising
   - for man on the street
3. **Citizen's National Bank**
   - handy locations
   - most progressive
4. **First Commercial Bank & Trust Co.**
   - aloof
   - rich man's bank

Since we attempted to obtain a cross section of business firms, it was possible to estimate the number of companies doing business with each major metropolitan bank The size of a bank is not always an accurate judge of the number of accounts it holds. One bank for instance had many more accounts than size alone would predict. Comparison of the data indicated that this was because a large number of companies with yearly sales of less than one million dollars tended to do business with that bank. We estimated the business market share of each of the banks in a way that gave our client new insights.

Our results indicated that some banks relied less on single bank customers than others did, the pattern of banking connections and reasons for them. Bank selection was influenced by such factors as age and size of company, location in relation to bank branches. This latter factor was of extreme importance in many cases.

Similarly, there was a wide variation in attitude towards the trust services of the various banks and the share of market in this category of bank service. The image of one of the banks made it seem less reliable for trust business than it might have expected. Image characteristics that attract retail and/or commercial business may affect some trust decisions negatively for certain categories of customers. For example, a bank with a conservative image might be much more successful in its trust department activities than the relevant public imagines.

A specially constructed technique was developed to measure strength of bank loyalty and predict future shifts in bank preferences. We found the image of the various banks to be a predictive factor in determining bank preferences for customers planning to change connections. However, there are a host of other variables that enter into the picture in determining ultimate choice of banking connection. The Security Trust had image problems of interest. Their own customers found the bank distasteful in some respects: "They feel they are so big that it doesn't matter if they take on your account or not." "They are pretty stiff and stuffy in their dealings." Of course, an attempt at being everybody's friend can also backfire into the distrust afforded those who seem to be glad-handing everybody in order to increase business. Colony Commercial was often placed in this role. As one man said "They are aggressive and have tried to sell themselves to the public . . . perhaps overly aggressive. Sometimes you don't like to deal with people who seem to be trying to push you into something." Another respondent was even more forceful. "Personally speaking, I don't like the Colony Commercial Bank. I just don't trust them; they would not do you any favor, unscrupulous, too fast-moving for me." Overall, Colony seemed to bear the brunt of the most negative comments that appeared in reference to personal service and treatment at the hands of loan officers. They were seen as having cold personnel and bankers who seemed to find it difficult to make the quick, sound decisions which the Colony advertising seemed to promise. An aggressive sales strategy can not only backfire, but if advertised promises are not backed up at the personal level in the bank itself, it can lead to even worse trouble. There are few more irate individuals than the businessman who was first wooed and then scorned. It seemed from the results of the survey that a little less reputation for friendliness might even be to a bank's advantage unless every member of the banking staff was prepared to behave cordially when it came to personal dealings with business customers.

When the material which we had collected pertaining to bank advertising was evaluated, it was important to remember that this study represented a cross-section of opinion at one point in time. Historically, metropolitan bank advertising had been carried out most actively by Security Trust and Colony Commercial. Citizen's had been promoting its services, especially over television, for a much shorter period of time. This was an important fact when attempting to evaluate the survey results in terms of awareness of advertising effectiveness and comparisons between various media used.

It was also necessary to bear in mind that at the time of this study (in the early sixties) advertising was just beginning to attempt to create a distinct image for the bank. As a result, most bank ads were relatively similar, and few businessmen paid much attention to them. What we were trying to determine, however, was whether Citizen's recent push into serious image-building was being noticed within the business community. To secure this information, each respondent was given specially designed attitude scales. The results were useful, but more information was needed.

It's nice to know that you're being seen, but it is more interesting to examine *how* the bank is being seen. To get information on the effectiveness of the advertisements, it was determined which bank's advertisements told its story best, which created the most curiosity about the bank, and which appealed most to businessmen. Bearing in mind the enormous resources of Security Trust and its fine reputation, the data showed Citizen's National was obviously gaining a place as a bank which could create memorable commercials.

The word "warmth" was considered as an indicator of emotional effectiveness, since a warm feeling generally implies receptiveness. In this case it would imply that the message was getting across very well. There were a lot of other questions dealing with bank advertisements, and when they were all combined in an index and averaged out, it provided accurate measurements of advertising effectiveness. These measures revealed that the advertising of Citizen scored significantly well, especially considering that two of the competitors were using much higher budgets for longer periods of time.

Overall Advertising Effectiveness

Security Trust	144
Citizens	121
Colony	75
First Commercial	46

As a final proof, respondents were asked which of Citizen's and Colony's advertisements made the greatest impression on them; of those who had seen the newspaper and television advertisements, most had better recall of the latter. The results of the survey had implications for both the advertising and the sales policies of the Citizen's National Bank, and neither one nor the other can be evaluated in isolation. The effectiveness of advertising for commercial banks is to a large extent measured by the way the advertising produces a receptive attitude for personal solicitation. It was likely that no metropolitan bank was utilizing personal solicitation as much as it might, and the psychological effects of being personally called on or called up by a bank cannot be underestimated. It enhances a businessman's opinion of himself more than any other type of selling can. As one financial manager reported "the president (of the local Colony branch) and the vice president keep after us even though we don't do business with them now . . . continually calling us to see if they can be of service."

Our interviews indicated that personal experiences and the opinions of friends are quite important to an individual as he forms an image of a bank. As one individual commented, "The smaller the bank, the closer you can get to the people in it." Another businessman was doing his banking with

Security Trust, but he was beginning to hear good things about Citizen's. "I have friends who do business with them," he said, " they are easier to do business with; sometimes they are a little more lenient and willing to take a chance on a person." Bearing in mind that this man had not done any business with Citizens, it underscores the importance of word of mouth. This man was actually quoting a friend of his, but he was expressing it as his own opinion. One bank, trying to be friendly in a too forceful manner will impress a businessman as hustling for a dollar whereas this same concern, when directed towards the customer in a warm and human manner, not only creates the feeling of closeness and concern, but turns the customer into a living advertisement for the bank.

When it comes to *word of mouth,* there should be definite attempts to utilize this most effective form of publicity. This does not mean standing on the corner regaling passers-by with the merits of your bank, or instructing the tellers to pass on the good word at their next cocktail party. There are certain groups of individuals who, for some reason or other, are considered more authoritative than most when it comes to financial advice from non-banking people. We suggest a special attempt to cater to accountants and attorneys, each of whom is usually highly regarded by his dozens of clients when it comes to prudent fiscal advice.

When it comes down to locating specific groups which would be most likely to welcome an association with Citizens, the survey gave some surprisingly direct indications. Also we were able to make some predictions as to what sorts of industries would be the most likely source of new accounts for Citizen's. Experience validated these predictions. Again, more specifically, we suggested a stepped up mailing effort, a system of telephone solicitation, and the development of leads. We also advised more work in the direction of pinpointing specific types of businesses and devised special ways of appealing to them. Humor in advertising would not be a dangerous thing either; subtle testing had revealed that many businessmen harbor unfriendly and hostile feelings towards banks as unwanted authority figures. With almost every other bank trying to outdo the others in a claim to strength and security, a bank which could tastefully poke fun at the common banking image, including itself, would make a favorable impression on a lot of people. We suggested how Citizen's might gain the additional image of the helpful teacher, concerned that the public understand banking more so it could make more use of its services.

All things taken into account, the Citizen's National Bank survey and study proved to be a useful tool providing much important and enlightening information to the bank officers. Now the Citizen's National Bank had a valuable inside lead; they knew just how the business community felt about them and their competitors. They had solid information as to what were their perceived strengths and weaknesses, and the perceived strengths and weaknesses of the other banks in their area. Both we and Citizen's were quite satisfied with the study, and we might add that in the last decade, Citizen's has chalked up a favorable growth rate, partially by implementing good banking practice with psychological know-how in dealing with the customers and the communities with which they do their work.

IX
INDUSTRIAL ENGINEERING FOR BANKS
by Robert J. Richmond

> Industrial Engineering is concerned with the design, improvement and installation of integrated systems of men, materials and equipment; it draws upon specialized knowledge and skill in the mathematical, physical and social sciences, together with the principles and methods of engineering analysis and design, to specify, predict, and evaluate the result obtained from such systems.*

This chapter will examine industrial engineering as it may be applied to banking in a broad sense. It will explore the various areas of bank involvement in industrial engineering in an effort to illuminate the potential benefits that may be expected.

The Function Of Industrial Engineering

Industrial engineering is a management tool; it serves as a unifying force in bringing together the knowledge and talents of the various scientific disciplines with those of business administration. A professionally staffed industrial engineering organization can integrate information from all functional areas to assist operations management in making decisions.

Industrial engineers 1) formulate, 2) analyze, 3) synthesize, 4) evaluate, 5) coordinate, 6) implement, and 7) monitor. This "scientific method" is used to solve a wide scope of problems in relation to everything from policy and procedure formulation to physical building projects and information flow pattern development. The end result of the industrial engineering function is profit improvement and operating efficiency.[1]

*American Institute of Industrial Engineers, Long Range Planning Committee, Industrial Engineering Seminars, Cornell University, 1955.
1. Maynard, H.B., Industrial Engineering Handbook, McGraw Hill, 2nd Edition 1963, Chapter 5, J, Keith Louden.

Industrial Engineering in Banking

Industrial engineering techniques are now being applied in many of the nations larger banking institutions and the various district offices of the Federal Reserve Bank.

The more classical applications of industrial engineering are commonly thought to be of use only in manufacturing situations — projects such as the layout of production machinery and the establishment of engineered performance standards for assembly operations in the auto industry, the application of work station planning and crew loading in an aircraft or electronics factory, or the design and implementation of materials handling and warehousing systems. However, the techniques applied to perform the needed functions for a production plant are just as applicable in a banking situation.

In banking systematic layout planning is of major importance. It is used to achieve an efficient flow of work in process, efficient use of allocated space and proper design of customer service areas. In any planning effort for the optimum arrangement of facilities, for personnel, operating equipment, storage space, materials handling or supporting services, or the development of design parameters for the best structure to contain these functions, the industrial engineer must gear his effort to the characteristics of the product or service to be supplied. In the case of banking, the product or main function can be described as "the internal and external transmission of information on a real time basis."

This overall system of information flow has four basic elements: collecting, processing, comparing, and selecting.[2] Information is transmitted, generated, recorded, evaluated, compiled, and manipulated by people and equipment. The people involved, for whom facilities, etc. must be provided, range from customers, to tellers, to computer engineers, to bank presidents. The machinery involved ranges from coin counters and tabulators, to security systems and even more sophisticated electronic devices. The vehicles of information flow, therefore, will logically vary from paper to currency, electronic impulses, microfilm, and mylar or paper tape. The physical handling of currency or negotiable certificates is by no means diminished in importance; although it is only a fractional portion of overall banking activities, it is, of course, part and parcel of the information flow, and is, in many cases, the most costly and time-consuming portion of the operation.

The projects presented below are indicative of the scope of tasks commonly handled by industrial engineers in the banking industry. This listing denotes

2. Ned Chapin, An Introduction to Automatic Computers, D. Van Nostrand Company, Inc., Princeton, N.J., 1957 P. 42.

projects undertaken in commercial, business, and Federal Reserve Banks: 1) Analysis of operating manuals, their revision and distribution; 2) reviews of all forms now in use and the type of reproduction used; 3) economical order quantities and desirable reorder points; 4) preparation of management reports or operating statistics; 5) monthly reports on the status of current capital equipment items and their budget commitments; 6) evaluations of equipment such as video tape machines, lineless telephones, 10 image per slide 35 mm film processing, new high speed offset reproduction systems; 7) queuing studies to define personnel needs in teller and customer service areas.

In addition, industrial engineers apply their techniques to aid the personnel function by designing training and education programs. Videotape lectures and "sound and slide" equipment are utilized. The industrial engineers are in most cases responsible for maintaining up-to-date floor plans for use in analysis of activity relationships. This type of study is essential during the analysis of space needs for the various departments as part of the design and layout of a new building. Studies of material handling, guard force training, and personnel identification systems have also been undertaken by industrial engineering groups. It is worthy to note that the name for these groups may vary from industrial engineering to planning, management engineering, or engineering services. Organizationally, they should report to the operations manager, or managing director at a relatively high level. This, of course, will vary depending upon each bank's internal structure, but the essential function and purpose will not change. Traditionally banks have not had "industrial engineering groups" as such, but have hired people with that background for various administrative positions in the management and decision-making process.

Industrial Engineering Methods and Techniques

Process flow charts are used by industrial engineers to track information flow. The term "process charts" refers to a family of charting techniques used for analytical purposes. These charts aid in detection and elimination of existing or potential inefficiencies in the direction and amount of flow of people, product, or information. The charts can be used for monitoring cycles of operations, transportations, and inspections as well as total storage and retrieval systems. They enable the observer to note (in some cases almost pictorially, as in flow diagrams) the functional relationships among various activities. For example, from such charted analyses of a "messenger — mail room" operation, one may ascertain whether activities can be combined or eliminated; whether the sequence of pickups may be restructured; or whether the time element, distribution, or distance involved may be changed to make the overall system flow more smoothly for factor discrimination of documents and information. Items which have been examined by these methods in various banks include draft notices, credit transfers, flow of incoming checks, check sorting, messenger routing, fleet truck delivery and pickup schedules, incoming customer correspondence; stock transfers, records accumulation and dispersal.

Man-machine charts or multiple activity charts are graphic representations used to coordinate the working and idle time of two or more workers, or any combination of machines, processors and operators of service personnel. The techniques involved are used in production planning to organize task cycles for more effective utilization of worker or machine time.

Activity relationship charts relate functional operations and their physical locations, cost, quality and quantity — both internal to their departments and external to the bank as a whole. The above mentioned items are by no means all of the methods used by industrial engineers, but are representative of those whose objective is to arrive at a timely cost-effective operation.

Forms, Design, and Control

The forms currently used by many banks for recording information (both customer recorded and employee recorded information) have not been designed for easy visibility of critical data and, in many instances, contain a good deal of extraneous information. This extra data is either used infrequently, if at all, is not required by law, or is duplicated on some other accessible document. The industrial engineers' background of knowledge includes human factors engineering which is readily useful in this area of forms design. Industrial engineers are also usually involved in the evaluation of programs for conversion of data from forms to punch cards or other input media for high speed electronic processing equipment. They also get involved in the various methods and economics of reproduction and distribution which are rapidly expanding in technology. Since time is of the essence in the business of banking, these areas are proving to be fruitful for study.

Work Management Programs

One of the most frequently mentioned areas where industrial engineering talent is being applied to banking is in programs of clerical work management. In this area, outside consulting firms have led the field. Analysis, evaluation, and development of standards for all clerical operations by industrial engineers has enabled management to predetermine the size of the work force necessary for specific highly repetitive tasks which are the life blood of bank operations. The industrial engineering group furnishes the accounting function with all the standards to be used in establishing costs and budgets. An important factor in these programs is the fact that banking by its very nature has perhaps more basic historical data available than most other forms of business. Since this data is available to an industrial engineering group it can be systematically arranged with the use of computers. It can then be statistically evaluated for the purpose of predicting workloads and analyzing transaction activity within departments during selected time spans; the standards can be applied and the budgets predicted with good reliability.

Work sampling studies, known for their effectiveness in assembly or process operations, can be practically applied to formulate the above mentioned standards for tabulating equipment, (in conjunction with the previously mentioned multiple activity charts) vacuum paper counters, coin wrapping machines, keypunch machines, teller services, and mailroom operations. Group timing techniques can be useful in determining the extent and nature of automation desirable or in determining machine downtime in automated areas. Statistical evaluations combining the sampling results and the machine downtime lead to predictions of equipment reliability and establishment of preventive and service maintenance policies. Knowledge of equipment reliability and system reliability is essential for a "real-time-dependent" operation such as banking.

Capital Equipment Justifications

Industrial engineers perform many services for long range or facilities planning. One such service is the evaluation and justification of the purchase of major capital equipment. This is usually done in the form of a "life cycle cost" study which, as the name implies, reviews and predicts the expenditures, savings generated, disposal value, labor and maintenance costs associated with the particular item over its useful life. Since technology is rapidly advancing and the "state of the art" of banking is changing, these analyses are important if the bank is to have the latest equipment to maintain a competitive advantage.

Many large banks with multi-branch operations have elected to maintain their own fleet of inter-division vehicles. Industrial engineers have been instrumental in determining as part of capital equipment justification studies, the type and sizes as well as the most cost effective schedules for their use. Evaluation of lease versus buy programs are also done by industrial engineers for equipment from trucks to computers.

Work Stations Analysis

The present security system now in use in most banks, consisting of a closed circuit T.V. system, can actually become a built-in reservoir of time — motion study data and queing data for the industrial engineers' use. This information, which can be obtained from specialized review of videotapes or 16 mm films, is valuable in analyzing different "work station" layouts under varying workload conditions in "real-time" situations. Analysis can be made of the effects of changing equipment or layout as well as changes in customer convenience activity areas.

Human Factors Engineering

In the areas of operation and customer contact, the industrial engineer brings to bear his knowledge of human factors data to assure that sizing and color of facilities (i.e. signs, table heights, teller windows, etc.) are efficient for employees on one hand and comfortable for the customer on the other. This is also the area where the industrial engineer can work with the market survey department or psychologist to create a particular image for the bank. The layout, illumination, furniture appointments, equipment, carpeting, security system, etc., will all contribute to that image.

Summary

The most important contribution of industrial engineering to banking is in the area of the management-decision making process. Managers of financial institutions are no different from managers of manufacturing plants in that they need factual information arranged to define and estimate the cost and consequences of alternative courses of action. The express purpose: to aid in solving existing or potential problems in either functional or customer contact areas.

The collection and arrangement of information, the emphasis of integration of the human elements into the system, the ability to predict and interpret statistical and economic data, and most of all, the concern with the total problem, i.e., the system approach; these are the factors which distinguish industrial engineering from other business or engineering disciplines. The industrial engineer is able to assist every level of bank management by originating and developing operating plans or programs, as well as the necessary means of analysis and control which permit cost effective use of human and economic resources.

Industrial engineering includes: systematic layout planning, predicting work loads and defining output, queing, analysis of sources of potential savings, and the areas of work design and management, to name a few. Simulation, or other use of computers, master planning safety, personnel administration, cost reduction programs, and training and educational programs also fall into category of areas in which industrial engineering can aid the functional departments in banking institutions today. The modern, professional industrial engineer provides solutions to problems before rather than after the fact; he provides creative assistance in support of dynamic modern management; and he provides factual and unbiased solutions based on his ability to measure, understand, simulate, and manipulate existing and future systems.

X

BANKERS AND THE COMMUNITY

At certain periods in history it is necessary to change in order to survive. Today we have large segments of society in despair, an inscrutable war that divides the country, racial animosities that produce alienation from society and anti-Establishment feelings, poverty, unemployment, and general economic conditions that baffle and weaken the entire business structure. In addition, families often don't prepare their children well for responsible adulthood, there is increased drug use, and attraction to binding community ties and religious traditions is on the wane. In the midst of this potential chaos, we maintain that the banking community offers society less than it must from both the points of view of long term and short term profitability. Community involvement is in the long range interest of banks. Bankers are traditionally aloof to social needs in human terms; they are *laissez-faire* in disposition. Social involvement is often restricted to the boards of large corporations, colleges, museums, and charities.

By nature, bankers shudder at unfavorable publicity. They don't take stands on public issues. In fact, leading bankers are sometimes known to endorse conservative positions on social matters such as restrictive housing and club discrimination, and to support, as private citizens, causes which are not in the public interest. On the other hand, bankers, more than any other group, can help unite the country and keep it stable, not only financially, but in the "quality of life." Let us examine some of the issues in this field.

The interview conducted by the Institute for Consumer Psychology with Melvin King of the Boston New Urban League — a leading figure in the Boston black community — is a good starting-off point. To him banks are the most important force in the well-being of the Negro community. "They exercise control over our economic development and the flow of resources, and they determine who gets what, but they have done practically nothing to help Blacks establish sound economic resources, nothing to counter the deterioration of the Boston schools, and nothing to openly question unfair practices of a mayor or school committee. Although they hire blacks for menial positions, there is no upgrading process, no effective mid-management training. . Banks should give large numbers of scholarships for blacks in colleges until there is free tuition at the state colleges and universities" [which he feels should be run on a two-shift basis to lessen admission problems] .

King suggests that the large banks organize "precinct development corporations" in the ghetto, organize black enterprise, train, provide venture capital and work diligently to improve the environment. King sees banks as exploiters of the black consumer: "They don't help black consumers become capitalists, they keep blacks consumers, not producers, or owners. . They play games with blacks asking for loans and figure the coolest way to turn them down, with various excuses about investment committees and overloaded resources." King also believes that about 20% of bank profits should be invested in the ghetto communities due to the present crisis. Especially disturbed about real estate progress, he feels that the savings banks have been hostile to black needs and should be taxed on their profits in the real estate field to force a pool of funds becoming available for community development. Also, savings bank life insurance should more easily be made available to black people, who now have little opportunity to learn about it, buy it, or benefit from its low-cost features. When discussing the refusal of the leading commercial banks to make any more student loans, Mr. King (considered one of the three or four most influential "over thirty-five" Blacks in Boston) stated bluntly: "If the banks refuse to help the kids, they should get clubs and force the banks to act as responsible community influences."

Let us turn from the black community to other areas of social concern. One of the largest banks in the country has less than one out of every $8000 of its assets in student loans and has discontinued such loans to "save money." An officer of this over $3-billion bank told the Institute that the bank loses at least 3% on each loan. The Institute computes the total revenue "lost" as less than ten percent of the bank's advertising budget. What goodwill does the bank receive from student loans? How much good will is it losing with its present policies?

The American Jewish Committee has published considerable material on the banking industry. This includes evidence of bank inactivity in upgrading Jewish employees and promotional decisions that are blatantly unfair to that minority group. Banks are weak on selling their calling as a career open to all minorities, and, in turn, they suffer from lack of qualified officers. The American Jewish Committee further reports that banks which hire highly talented Jews keep them in the "back room" in research and away from non-Jewish customers because they attribute "an Einstein syndrome" to

Jewish middle management. However, many banks are prone to have at least one prominent Jewish director and occasionally a customer-calling officer to help gain certain types of clients. Disconcerting is the report of the AJC that in New York City, with a Jewish population of 25%, about one percent of the bankers (officers and middle management) are Jewish, and ninety percent of the banks do not have even one Jewish officer. Savings banks were found somewhat different, with 2.5% Jewish officers. The situation nationally is similar, and banking is still a field in which Jews feel unwelcome.

Another social area of some interest is the relation of banks to large industry, which can borrow at the prime rate of interest. Minority groups, usually representing smaller and more risky enterprises, obviously pay higher interest for loans, although bias is not the main factor; banks should be very reluctant to deny loans to members of minority groups and should keep their interest charges reasonable. Blacks often resort to the 18% charge cards and to revolving credit which forces them to pay more for their money. The Institute found a case of a Negro who, when refused a loan, threatened to tell about it on a radio talk show; the bank quickly made the loan. There is little to be baffled about when Ralph Nader announces his entry into banking, and this should cause the banking industry to pause, study, evaluate, communicate with the public, and become more solidly agreeable to taking an active role in uniting a divided and unhappy country. No other industry can do more to make this country sound, not only economically, but socially and morally.

Otherwise, they are some unpleasant predictions of things to come: increases in social discord; radical attacks on banks and the banking system; and the application of activist techniques to banks. It would be judicious for banks to anticipate the future and turn the present social malaise into a profit-making challenge rather than a source of possible anxiety about the present and the future.

XI
CONCLUDING COMMENTS

Many articles have appeared recently in banking and financial trade journals which have asked the question "Why are banks unreceptive to marketing research," or "Why do some banks still reject a marketing approach as part of their business procedure." In this book, we have attempted to answer some of these questions in a manner which we have tried to make as clear as possible. Asking these leading questions is a sure bait to attract the interest of a bank officer, but usually the articles simply pose the problem. Without a comfortable knowledge of the various areas of marketing, it is easy to dismiss such approaches as innapropriate or ineffectual. Therefore, we have purposely limited the scope of this work so that it will serve as an introduction to a technique rather than a light discussion of all the many areas in which the utilization of these techniques could bring positive results. We have tried, moreover, to help discover the reasons that some bankers may well be unresponsive to certain business methods, and we have provided some suggestions at to why bank customers might also be unresponsive to appeals which might seem effective and appropriate to a financial officer.

In this concluding chapter, we will lightly touch upon a few areas which have been of particular interest to the Institute for Consumer Psychology, areas which have not been fully researched, but seem to offer good possibilities for constructive action.

One very important area of banking is the overseeing of private trusts. The trust department may be the least visible to the business or retail customer, but it is always an important source of revenue for the commercial bank or trust company. Unfortunately, the rise in the living standard in this country, and the concurrent rise in the number of people with a higher discretionary income, has prompted the emergence of many investment opportunities of a relatively safe nature. Life insurance, funding programs (formerly only active in California but rapidly gaining in popularity), and literally hundreds of respectable mutual fund groups now actively compete for the invested dollar. It is rather unlikely that a large number of recipients of trusts would be likely to attempt to dissolve them and play the stock market with the resultant capital. It is much more likely, however, that the individual who has amassed a portfolio of mutual funds would be likely to trust in the management of the fund to maintain and diversify his investment base. We have repeatedly stressed that the cornerstone of the banking profession lies in the concept of security, for both the good and the harm that this concept does to the profession. It was natural, then, for those who wished to have their funds administered carefully to literally trust in a trust department to carry out this duty. Since the objective was a guaranteed payback over a long period of time, it was logical to go to a conservative financial institution to find this sort of service.

The emergence of the mutual fund has, however, caused a considerable shift in the attitudes of a great many people. In their attempts to try to do away with the image of the stock market speculator, many mutual funds have actively portrayed themselves as stable, careful, and dependable. On top of this, moreover, they point to the rising economy of the country and offer the possibility of considerable capital growth over a period of time. It is this growth potential which, although not spelled out in black and white, is causing the rapid increase in both the number and size of mutual funds. Previously, the main cause for concern was whether the money was safe. A generation of Americans who has either weathered the depression or had been close enough to be well aware of its affects had a psychological concern for the safekeeping of cash and perhaps a bit of mistrust for the stock market. Forty years has gone by, however, and there is currently an adult generation which has known nothing of such financial trauma. They have seen the economy of a seemingly endless upward path (until 1970). Bearing in mind the regulations which were instituted after the crash and the internationalization of the economy which has occurred in the last twenty-five years, it seems reasonable to expect this economic growth to continue for at least the forseeable future. In other words, the fund managers are in many cases offering the same security as the trust department, while taking advantage of the economic climate to influence possible investors to trust in the mutual fund's management.

Since mutual funds, stockbrokers and bank trust departments are basically in the same business, that of maintaining a customers portfolio of invested income, there is no real reason why a trust department shouldn't utilize the same techniques which have proven to be so successful for other portfolio managers. This notion will of course, be met with a certain number of raised eyebrows, but it is common sense to realize that the young man who is on his way to the top is not likely to want to turn to a bank trust department when he feels he has been more than adequately taken care of by his mutual fund investments. And the wives of these men will be the little old ladies of the 1980's and 90's.

There are many ways in which the public could be informed of the work of the trust department. More than that, each large bank has one, so any person with a suitable amount of capital or funds to put into a trust fund will have the actual fund manager as a relatively close personal connection. The concept may sound at this point to be a little too brash, but the idea of the efficient, quick fund manager combined with the stability already associated with a bank administered trust is a very positive combination. Although the Institute has not yet prepared a full scale study of this opportunity, we already feel that it would not be very difficult to offer the trust department's services to large account holders much in the same manner as a financial counselor or a stock advisor. This in turn would present the bank's trust department as a logical alternative when that account holder decided to turn over the administration of his invested capital to another party, be it a broker, a fund, or a bank. Again we are stressing the image of a bank as being a full-service financial center. The bank is already capable of fulfilling a number of functions for various types of customers, but too often, a customer sees his bank in only one role.

Because of the tendency of a customer to type his bank as a checking account, or a place to borrow money, or the administrator of Grannie's trust fund, many valuable opportunities to increase service are often missed. The Institute for Consumer Psychology recently did some work in the area of cross-selling as applied to retail banking. The most interesting result of the investigations, from a psychological viewpoint, was the lack of cross-selling evidenced in most banks which had co-operated with the survey. Customers would come to a bank with a set idea of what service they were seeking, and would generally be satisfied by locating just that one service. There was really no attempt on the part of the bank, aside from a few signs and a brochure generally describing the services available, to interest the customer in the other areas in which the bank might be of help. In mutual savings banks, which in Massachusetts function as agencies for Savings Bank Life Insurance, there was insufficient effort to determine whether or not a new customer would be a suitable prospect for increased insurance protection. Commercial banks also often had no way of determining whether a new customer, retail or commercial, would be in the market for some other financial service which the bank could provide.

The Institute survey concluded that the teller, the person who comes in contact with the customer most often could be very helpful if he, or she, could make polite suggestions as to various banking services while actually helping the customer. This concept was often hard to implement, since many tellers, anxious to rise up the ladder in the bank, were already emulating the friendly yet reserved attitude which we have found often characterizes so many bank officers. The tellers, like bank officers, did not want to act in the capacity of salesmen, although they, more than any other employees of the bank, were in constant contact with the new and the regular customers.

Besides developing some training aids to help tellers become representatives of the bank, the Institute also came up with an information card which unobtrusively elicited certain types of information about each new customer. These cards could be data-coded and card-sorted to provide a basic mailing or calling list which would pinpoint the customers who would be most receptive to a life-insurance plan, a home-improvement loan, or even a vacation travel loan.*

Going further with the concept of "segmenting the market," the Institute began to develop specific programs to be aimed at specific retail markets, such as teenagers, young adults, and housewives. The last category is especially important when one realizes the number of women who are regular retail customers of the average bank. Despite their numbers they are relatively neglected as an important and reachable audience for specific, segmented marketing appeals. Women are beginning to be recognized, however, as evidenced by the recent election of the first female vice-president of the American Institute for Banking and the implementation of marketing programs in several large banks aimed at both attracting more female customers while at the same time educating them and informing them of how their bank can be of service to them. Here, especially, the techniques of surveys and psychological analysis can be of great help, since banking has been traditionally a masculine-dominated profession, even more than most others. When a bank in Virginia conducted a limited survey, however, and discovered that women were "involved" (both single names and joint accounts) in 57% of the total checking accounts and 64% of the total dollar deposits, it quickly began to formulate an action program to become more responsive to this market. The bank had a widely publicized "Ladies Day." Each office worked up a variation on the theme with materials, posters, and booklets provided by the Women's Department and marketing staff of the central office. Some of the smaller branch offices had coffee hours of soft drinks for the lobby customers of the day. All give favors, including gaily

The Institute has available at nominal cost a training manual for humanized bank marketing, a portfolio of survey forms and a sample research tape recording of a group interview.

colored shopping bags. An unexpected result was the fact that some men customers took the shopping bags as well. One man was heard to say "It's exactly what my wife needs, she's always dropping packages." Thus, a segmented appeal based on the psychological needs of various minority customers will often have unexpected dividends in the form of increased awareness among other groups who, seeing that the bank is making a specific appeal to a specialized audience, realize that they too may be afforded the same sort of personalized service.

Needless to say, banking is rapidly becoming a profession of financial service sensitive to the ever-growing needs of all segments of the economy and the population. As our nation becomes richer, benefiting from the fruits of technological advance, the need for dependable financial assistance will become increasingly greater. As our nation grows in its social awareness, more and more people will require the services of banks and financial institutions to help them save, invest, borrow or simply facilitate their day-to-day financial dealings.

There was a time when the only persons that the banker had to be really sensitive to were the large businessman, the large investor, the auditors. The world moves on, though, and it is becoming increasingly important to become sensitive to a wide variety of types of people, all of whom can become valuable customers in one capacity or another.

To achieve an emotional sensitivity to a personality type not one's own is a difficult if not almost an impossible task, but it is a task which can be immensely eased by good, relevant information on the wants and expectations of many types of people. For years, general retail establishments have had to deal with this situation, but the financial profession really does not have the long history of dealing with many heterogenous personality types.

It is not appropriate for the psychologist to advise people on financial matters. Nor would it be fitting for a financial officer to turn his attention solely to the understanding of human motivations. Together, however, the two professions can help create a banking community responsive to all segments of the business and retail market, limited in growth only by the limits of imagination.